HANDICAPS OF CHILDHOOD

First published 1921
This edition published by Lector House in 2024

ISBN: 978-93-6138-366-3

Lector House LLP
Registered Office: H. No. 96, Block C, Tomar Colony,
Burari, Delhi – 110084, India
info@lectorhouse.com
www.lectorhouse.com

HANDICAPS OF CHILDHOOD

HENRY ADDINGTON BRUCE

2024

LECTOR HOUSE LLP

HANDICAPS OF CHILDHOOD

BY

H. ADDINGTON BRUCE

Author of "Psychology and Parenthood," "The Riddle of Personality," etc.

TO MY FATHER
JOHN BRUCE
IN LOVING REMEMBRANCE OF BOYHOOD
JOYS AND ADVANTAGES

PREFACE

It is my hope that this book will be read as a companion-volume to "Psychology and Parenthood," it being designed to amplify and supplement that earlier work. Its general aim, accordingly, is to present additional evidence in support of the central doctrine of "Psychology and Parenthood,"—namely, that, in view of the discoveries of modern psychology with regard to individual development, the mental and moral training of children by their parents ought to be begun earlier, and be carried on more intensively, than is the rule at present. But whereas in "Psychology and Parenthood" the emphasis was chiefly on the importance of early mental training, the chief concern of the present book is to demonstrate the importance of early training in the moral sphere.

Everybody, of course, is more or less aware that lifelong character defects may result from parental neglect to develop in children such qualities as unselfishness, self-confidence, and self-control. But few really appreciate that, by this neglect, children are burdened with handicaps which, persisting into adult life, may imperil not alone the winning of success and happiness, but health itself. And, among parents, comparatively few are sufficiently alert to the danger signals giving warning that such handicaps of perhaps catastrophic significance are being needlessly imposed on their children. Eccentricities of behaviour in children—such as jealousy and sulkiness—are too often ignored as being of no particular account, or are sadly misinterpreted by parents, with perhaps dire consequences to the children's whole careers.

These eccentricities and their possible consequences, these danger signals and handicaps, form in the main the subject-matter of the pages that follow. Desiring the book to be helpful to as many people as possible, I have been careful to avoid writing in any technical scientific way, and have tried to be simple and concrete. For this reason many illustrative cases from real life are given, my belief being that I could thus present most convincingly the truly remarkable facts with which the successive chapters have to deal. The result, I sincerely trust, will be to contribute in some degree to save children from the handicaps in question, and to assist adults now afflicted with any of these handicaps to overcome them.

In large part, this book has already appeared in the columns of several magazines. To the editors of these magazines—*The Century Magazine, Good Housekeeping Magazine, McClure's Magazine, Harper's Bazar, Every Week,* and *The Mother's Magazine*—I owe grateful acknowledgment for the opportunity to acquaint their readers with the discoveries and theories herein set forth. I am also under a debt of gratitude to numerous psychological and medical friends for advice and information. And, as in the case of all my previous books, I am particularly indebted to my wife for inspiration, encouragement, and innumerable helpful suggestions.

H. ADDINGTON BRUCE.

Cambridge, Massachusetts,
July, 1917.

CONTENTS

CHAPTER I

MENTAL BACKWARDNESS

ONCE upon a time, not many years ago, a distinguished French psychologist paid a visit to a Parisian public school. It was accounted an excellent school, and its principal beamed with pardonable pride when the visiting psychologist, Doctor Alfred Binet, explained that he would like to see the pupils at work. Forthwith his desire was granted, and for a time he attentively followed the exercises of a class of forty children. He said little by way of comment, until, toward the close of the lesson-hour, he abruptly inquired:

"Which of these pupils do you consider the most intelligent?"

"That boy yonder," the master answered, nodding toward a pleasant-faced youngster who was diligently reading his book.

"And, pray, how old is he?"

"He is twelve."

"That, I suppose, is the average age for the class?"

"Well, no. I should say that they are on the average ten years old."

"What, then, is this twelve-year-old boy doing among them? If he is so bright, why is he lingering among these little ones? My dear sir," the psychologist continued, while the principal stood in abashed silence, "would it not be nearer the mark to call him a backward instead of a bright child? And would it not be well to search for the cause of his backwardness and try to remedy it? Assuredly, this boy should constitute for you a delicate problem that insistently demands solution."

This, I say, happened not many years ago. For that matter, incidents quite like it occasionally happen even to-day, testifying to the inability of some teachers to appreciate the presence, let alone the significance, of the laggard in the schoolroom. But in the brief period that has elapsed since Alfred Binet began his epoch-making investigations in the schools of Paris, there has undoubtedly been a genuine and widespread awakening in respect to the tremendously important problem raised by the backward child. Especially is this true of our own land. Nowhere else, perhaps, have more diligent efforts been made to ascertain the extent and causes of backwardness among the school-going population, and nowhere else is greater activity being displayed in the beneficent task of transforming the backward child, as far as possible, into the normal one.

Certainly, too, it must regretfully be added that there is abundant reason for this activity. Researches conducted during the past ten years by American school authorities and by independent investigators, have revealed an appalling state of affairs. Doctor Oliver P. Cornman, a district superintendent of the Philadelphia schools, making a statistical survey of five city school systems, found 21.6 per cent. of Boston school children a year or more behind the normal grade for their age; 30 per cent. behind grade in New York; 37.1 per cent. behind grade in Philadelphia; 47.5 per cent. behind grade in Camden, New Jersey; and 49.6 per cent. behind grade in Kansas City. Doctor Leonard P. Ayres, acting in behalf of the Russell Sage Foundation, investigated fifteen New York City public schools, having twenty thousand pupils, and found a degree of retardation ranging from 10.9 per cent. to 36.6 per cent. Scrutiny of the school reports of more than thirty other cities revealed an average retardation of 33.7 per cent. Taking this as a fair average for the whole country, we have a total of between six and seven million American school children who are a year and more behind grade.

To be sure, this does not mean that all these children are intellectually deficient, for the term "retarded" is by no means synonymous with "dullards." Irregular attendance owing to illness or truancy accounts for not a little retardation. The education of a good many children is deliberately postponed by their parents, and as a result they are necessarily behind grade for some time after they enter school. In the case of many others, especially in cities like New York and Boston, where there is a large foreign-born population, ignorance of the English language is a sufficient cause for temporary retardation. Thus, I have received a letter from Doctor William H. Maxwell, superintendent of schools, New York City, in which he points out that many New York school children are recently arrived immigrants, coming from a foreign country, considerably above the age at which school-going usually begins. The personal inefficiency of teachers is also a factor to be reckoned with. Many a child becomes a "repeater" simply because he has had a poor teacher.

Nevertheless, when every possible allowance is made, the results of the investigations by Doctor Ayres, Superintendent Cornman, and their co-workers sum up to a deplorable showing. It is a showing, however, with one distinctly redeeming feature. Readers of my previous book, "Psychology and Parenthood," will remember it was there pointed out that the proportion of juvenile delinquents who are "born bad," and for whom no remedial measures will avail, is exceedingly small. There is reason for saying precisely the same thing with regard to the retarded child.

He may be dull, stupid, to all appearance hopelessly defective, but the researches of the past decade, the fruits of the mind-developing experiments that have gone apace with the discovery of the extent to which backwardness prevails, leave no doubt that in most cases the child who is a true dullard may be brought almost, if not fully, to normal intellectual activity, provided he is taken in hand at an early day. In fact, even the most pessimistically inclined investigators admit that, at an outside estimate, not more than 2 per cent. of backward children are backward because of incurable defects of the brain. Many present-day authorities put the figure as low as 1 per cent., and my own belief is that even this is too high a proportion.

Undoubtedly—and especially since the invention of psychological tests to determine the mental state of dullards—many children have been erroneously pronounced feeble-minded when their backwardness is in reality due to remediable causes. The trouble is not with the tests so much as with the inexperience of those who apply them, some of the tests being seemingly so easy of application that in many instances they have been utilised by teachers and others having little or no training in clinical psychology. This is particularly true concerning the application of the much-talked-about Binet-Simon method of mental diagnosis, devised by Doctor Alfred Binet and his colleague in scientific child study, Professor Simon.

The Binet-Simon method is certainly simple enough, and, rightly used, is of great value. It was formulated by putting to hundreds of children, ranging in age from three to thirteen, a series of questions and commands of increasing difficulty, noting the results obtained, and selecting as "norms" for each age the questions and commands to which the majority of the children of that age were able to respond correctly. Thus it furnishes a convenient means for determining with considerable accuracy the degree of mental retardation of any particular child. Experience has shown, though, that its fixed standard, by which children are pronounced "mentally defective" if they fall three years behind the norm for their age, is not always an infallible guide. When the method is applied by the untrained investigator the result is sometimes absurd.

For instance, in one American city 49.7 per cent. of six hundred retarded children tested by the Binet-Simon method were reported as being "feeble-minded," while 80 per cent. of three hundred children in the special classes of another city school system were similarly stigmatised. On such a basis we should have, among the six million retarded children in our schools, from three to nearly five million who are feeble-minded. Even if the Binet-Simon testing is done by an expert, there is always the danger of incorrect diagnosis, with resultant serious injustice to the child tested, unless the indications drawn from the testing are verified by careful clinical and laboratory investigation. A few cases from the experience of a well-known clinical psychologist, Doctor J. E. Wallace Wallin, director of the Psycho-Educational Clinic, Board of Education, St. Louis, may well be cited to illustrate and emphasise this important truth.

There was once brought to Doctor Wallin a pupil in a private school, an attractive girl of seventeen, who was studying—or, rather, attempting to study—Latin, history, algebra, and English. Her teacher complained that she could remember little or nothing of what was taught her, that her attention flagged easily, and that in other ways she did not seem to be of normal mentality. And, in fact, tested by the Binet-Simon method she graded only eleven and a half years old.

Had the psychological inquiry into her condition stopped there, she would have been declared a fit subject for institutional care, according to the Binet-Simon rating. But Doctor Wallin insisted on additional and different testings, and presently made the significant discovery that her trouble lay, not in any structural brain defect, but in a functional weakness of the nervous system that caused her to become fatigued at slight mental exertion. She was, in short, a "psychasthenic," and needed only proper treatment by a skilled neurologist to be put into condition to profit from her lessons as her schoolmates did.

So, too, with a man of twenty-eight, who, tested by the Binet-Simon system, displayed the mentality of a boy of twelve. Had he been in the hands of an investigator who knew no more of the technic of psychological examination than the Binet-Simon scale, he would unhesitatingly been classified as feeble-minded. But, as Doctor Wallin said, in discussing the case:

"He did not impress me at all as being feeble-minded. His appearance, speech, and conduct suggested the polished and cultivated gentleman. I put him through approximately thirty sets of mental tests [other than twenty-five individual Binet tests] and thirty moral tests. These tests demonstrated that there was a considerable difference in the strength of his different mental traits. Some traits were on the twelve-year plane, some on the fifteen-year, and some on the adult plane. In some mental tests he did as well as college men. He passed correctly practically all of the moral tests.

"His was indeed a case showing more or less deficiency in respect to various mental traits. But, contrary to the Binet rating, the man was not feeble-minded. It eventually developed that a sexual complex was at the root of his trouble."

Again, with the express purpose of determining the reliability or unreliability of the Binet-Simon tests as sufficient indicators of the mental status, Doctor Wallin applied these tests to several successful farmers and business men. The results were surprising and amusing. He tells us:

"The 1908 scale was administered according to my own Guide,[1] and the 1911 according to Goddard's version, which is usually used in this country for diagnosing feeble-mindedness. The subjects were generously rated in the tests; i.e., full credit was given for some responses that did not quite meet the technical passing requirements. Measured by the standards of one of the best rural communities of the country, socially and industrially considered, and by my own intimate knowledge of the subjects tested during the greater part of my life, not a single one of these persons could by any stretch of the imagination be considered feeble-minded. Not a single one has any record of delinquency, or crime, petty or major, or indulges in alcoholic beverages. All are law-abiding citizens, eminently successful in their several occupations, all except one (who is unmarried) being parents of intelligent, respectable children. The heredity is entirely negative, except for a few cases of minor nervous troubles and alcoholic addiction. No relative in the first or second generation, so far as it was possible to get the facts by inquiry, was ever committed to a penal institution or an institution for the mentally defective or disordered."

Yet, given the Binet-Simon tests, every member of this group, if judged by the tests alone, would have to be rated as feeble-minded. Here is Doctor Wallin's account of one of these most illuminating cases:

"Mr. A., sixty-five years old, faculties well preserved, attended school only about three years in the aggregate; a successful farmer and later a successful busi-

[1] As given in J. E. Wallace Wallin's "Experimental Studies of Mental Defectives," 1912, p. 116 *et seq*.

ness man, now partly retired on a competency of $30,000 (after considerable financial reverses from a fire); for ten years president of the board of education in a town of seven hundred; superintendent or assistant superintendent of a Sunday school for about thirty years; bank director; raised and educated a family of nine children, all normal; one engaged in scientific research (Ph.D.), one assistant professor in a state agricultural school, one assistant professor in a medical school (now completing thesis for Sc.D.), one a former music teacher and organist, a graduate of a musical conservatory, now an invalid; one a graduate of the normal department of a college, one a graduate nurse, two engaged in a large retail business, one holds a clerical position, all high-school graduates, and all, except one, one-time students in colleges and universities.

"Failed on all the new 1911 tests except six digits and suggestion lines (almost passed the central-thought test). In the 1908 scale, passed all the ten-year tests and some higher tests. Binet-Simon age, 1908, 10.8; retardation, fifty-four years; intelligence quotient, .17. According to the 1912 scale, 10.6 years."

Doctor Wallin fittingly comments:

"This man, measured by the automatic standards now in common use, would be hopelessly feeble-minded (an imbecile by the intelligence quotient) and should have been committed to an institution for the feeble-minded long ago. But is there any one who has the temerity, in spite of the Binet 'proof,' to maintain, in view of this man's personal, social, and commercial record, and the record of his family, that he has been a social and mental misfit and an undesirable citizen, and should, therefore, have been restrained from propagation because of mental deficiency (his wife is still less intelligent). No doubt, if a Binet tester had diagnosed this man forty or fifty years ago, he would have had him colonised as a 'mental defective.' It is a safe guess that there are hundreds of thousands like him throughout the country, no more intelligent and equally successful and prudent in the management of their affairs. Had he been a criminal when he was tested, the Binet testers who implicitly follow these standards would have offered 'expert testimony' under oath that he was feeble-minded and unable to distinguish between right and wrong, or unable to choose the right and avoid the wrong."

Truly, feeble-mindedness in an adult or child is not safely to be determined by relying merely on the results of a set of stereotyped mental tests. On the other hand, in deciding as to a child's actual mental state it is far more misleading to depend on unaided observation as a guide. Yet, since the beginning of scientific investigation into the causes of backwardness, cases have continually been coming to light in which teachers and even parents have mistakenly identified curable dullness with incurable feeble-mindedness, and have abandoned all effort at intellectual development. Sometimes, consequently, a condition closely resembling outright idiocy results from sheer neglect, as in one particularly striking case, for knowledge of which I am indebted to Doctor Arthur Holmes of Pennsylvania State College, well known for his work in clinical psychology.

In this case the daughter of a well-to-do professional man failed to show normal growth in infancy and was supposed by her sorrowing father to be weak-minded.

Left to her own devices, on the theory that it would be useless to try to mend the work of Providence, she remained until the age of eight in a state of seeming imbecility. She could not read or write, could not speak more than three words, and spent most of her time gibbering in a corner. Then, as good fortune would have it, she came under the observation of an expert investigator of mental conditions and was subjected for a year to careful training. At the end of that time she "could speak in simple sentences, answer ordinary questions intelligently, read in a primer, write a few words, and conduct herself in the manner of a little lady."

In other words, she had been taken in hand in time to save her from a life of incompetency, misery, and mental darkness. Is it not reasonable to infer, in the light of this and similar cases on record, that our institutions for the feeble-minded would be far less crowded than they are to-day had regenerative measures been likewise applied to their inmates in early childhood? Indeed, with Professor Lightner Witmer, dean of American clinical psychologists, I am prepared to affirm:

"I believe that a child may be feeble-minded in one environment—for example, in his own home—and may cease to exhibit feeble-mindedness when placed in a different environment. I also agree with those modern students of insanity who assert that the development of some forms of insanity may be averted by a proper course of discipline and training. Analogously, I contend that because a child of sixteen or twenty presents a hopeless case of feeble-mindedness, this is no evidence that proper treatment instituted at an earlier age might not have determined an entirely different course of development."

Also, as in the case of the criminal alleged to have been "born bad," mental backwardness has again and again been found to depend on comparatively slight physical defects—defects of eye, ear, mouth, nose, throat, teeth—the correction of which often results in a spontaneous and remarkable intellectual awakening.[2] Or the dullness mistaken for feeble-mindedness may be due to a generally weakened physical condition, the result of unhygienic home surroundings, lack of outdoor exercise, poor food, and so forth. Here is a case in point, reported by Professor Witmer. It is the case of a little Philadelphia girl, Fannie, the eight-year-old daughter of Russian-Jewish parents, whose two-room home is thus described by Professor Witmer:

"The living-room had one window, and contained a table, a few chairs, a stove, a lounge, dirty clothes piled in one corner, a barking cur, and many flies. The table was covered with a piece of black oilcloth, and on this were usually to be found pieces of brown bread and glasses of tea. No meals were prepared and the family never sat down to table. Their diet consisted chiefly of bread, tea, and sometimes fish. The bread was always on the table for the flies to crawl over and the children to eat when their hunger drove them to it.

"The front of the house looked out on a board fence which divided a double alley. In the rear was a small back yard. One hydrant at the entrance sufficed for the different families. There was underground drainage, but an offensive odour came from the closets. This was the soil in which Fannie had struggled to grow

[2] For some illustrative cases see "Psychology and Parenthood," especially pp. 174-178.

for eight years. When the school nurse visited the house, Fannie sat crouched in a corner, her eyes sullen and dead, her mouth hanging open, her skin showing the poorly nourished condition. Her eyes were crossed, her teeth irregular, the whole face devoid of life or interest.

"Fannie had been two years in the first grade of a Philadelphia school, and had made in that time so little progress that there was no possibility of promoting her to the next grade at the end of that school year. During the first year her attendance had been somewhat irregular, but despite the regular attendance of the second year she had profited little, and had come to be overlooked because she was thought to be too feeble-minded to progress in a school for normal children."

Taken to the psychological clinic, she was given a thorough physical and mental examination. She was found to be afflicted both with adenoid growths and enlarged tonsils, and was sent to a hospital to be operated on for these. Later she was entered in the hospital school connected with Professor Witmer's clinic at the University of Pennsylvania. Here she remained a year, part of that time attending also one of the city's public schools. Both mentally and morally she made satisfactory progress. Her sullenness rapidly disappeared under sympathetic handling. Though "at first she did not seem to understand affection," by the end of six weeks "she was the most demonstratively affectionate child in the school." Professor Witmer adds:

"During the first summer she appeared extremely sluggish. She showed very little tendency to play, and preferred to sit more or less motionless. As good food, better air, sunlight, and kindly treatment began to take effect, she burst forth with such excessive vitality, such exuberant spirits, that once when I had her before the psychological clinic one of the teachers asked if the lively movements were not the result of St. Vitus's Dance. This first outburst of vitality gradually subsided, leaving her a normally active child."

Undeniably, of course, even though a vicious household environment was chiefly responsible for this girl's backwardness, the adenoids and enlarged tonsils were also responsible for it in some degree. Parents cannot too keenly appreciate the hurtful effect bodily defects like these may have on mental development. Doctor Ayres, who has made an exhaustive study of this factor in retardation, estimates that it alone accounts for about 9 per cent. of the laggards in our schools, and clinical psychologists are disposed to put the percentage still higher. On the other hand, their experience with retarded children has led them to the important conclusion that, helpful as spectacles, the ear syringe, and the surgeon's knife may be, "after-treatment" in the form of careful individual training usually is indispensable, if only for the reason that while handicapped by the bodily defect the child may have acquired faulty mental habits which need to be corrected before education by ordinary schoolroom methods can count for much.

This means, manifestly, that many agencies must co-operate in the regeneration of the curable dullard. How many are sometimes involved may perhaps be sufficiently indicated by detailing another case from Professor Witmer's extensive experience, the case of an eleven-year-old boy who was brought to the University of Pennsylvania's psychological clinic with a history of five wasted years in school.

Any suspicion that this boy might belong to the ranks of the truly feeble-minded was dissipated by the results of the exhaustive mental testing through which Professor Witmer put him. This showed not only that he was naturally intelligent, but also that he was of an affectionate, generous, and thoughtful disposition. When, however, a physical examination was made, ample reason for his dullness was discovered, for it was found that he was suffering from adenoids, enlarged tonsils, weakness of vision, and dental trouble, his teeth being decayed and unclean, with tartar pushing back the gums, which were inflamed and swollen. In addition, he was stoop-shouldered, had an irregular heart action, and showed signs of being poorly nourished.

"Before anything can be done to improve your boy's mental state," it was explained to his mother, "his physical condition will have to be improved. He should be put under treatment without delay."

Then began a distressful period for the hapless youngster. First of all, a throat specialist operated on him for the removal of the adenoids and the hyper-trophied tonsils. After this he was sent to the eye clinic, where he was fitted with glasses. Next, he was taken to the dental clinic, where his teeth were cleaned and filled. All the while a trained social worker kept in touch with his parents to make sure that he would receive the hygienic care which had hitherto been wanting. In the meantime, he was allowed to return to school, from which, after the beginning of the summer vacation, he was transferred to a special school for backward boys. Here he remained most of the summer, being given individual attention with regard to his mental and physical needs.

It was noticed at first he was inclined to be quick-tempered and disorderly; but under the tactful handling he received he soon settled down. From being puny and delicate, he became an active, vigorous boy, excelling in the swimming-pool and the gymnasium. At his books he also made such progress that, on returning to regular school in the autumn, he was promoted through two grades in less than six months, being then only one grade behind normal and giving every promise of catching up with the boys of his own age in another six months.

Altogether, the services of half a dozen specialists in psychology, medicine, and education, and the expenditure of much time, effort, and money had been required to get this boy straightened out. Nor is his by any means an uncommon case. Moreover, like the case of the gibbering girl of eight, it illustrates another point in connection with the problem of retardation which should indeed be emphasised—the part played by parental ignorance and thoughtlessness in swelling the army of the retarded.

Had the parents of this boy appreciated the close relationship between bodily health and the health of the mind, had they taken alarm at the first signs of malnutrition and sought the advice of a competent physician, instituting developmental measures in accordance with his counsel, their son might not have become an educational "lame duck," and all the tedious and costly restorative work of later years would then have been avoided. To be sure, it must immediately be added that maintenance of his physical health would not of itself have unfailingly operated as a guarantee against retardation.

For, quite conceivably, he might have been surrounded by an intellectually deadening home environment, receiving from his parents neither proper disciplining nor encouragement and stimulus to mental activity, with the result that when the time came for him to go to school he would display little capability for, or interest in, the tasks of the classroom. So frequently is this actually the case that students of retardation are inclining more and more to rate faulty home training as perhaps the chief cause of mental backwardness. Thus we find one keen observer, Professor P. E. Davidson, declaring in an address at an educational convention in California:

"Parental neglect as a cause, resulting in emotional and volitional disorder, is emphasised in our cases. Learning in school is conditioned largely by what Witmer calls 'pedagogical rapport,' wherein a deference to the prestige of the teacher and the school and a sensitiveness to its rewards and punishments are such as rapidly to produce a habit of voluntary effort or active attention. Confirmed wilfulness at home and undisciplined impulsiveness must undoubtedly figure in the matter of learning. If the child's organic habit, after five or six years of poor home training, makes avoidance of the painfulness of effort the usual thing, we may be sure the teacher in the first grade will have unusual difficulty in inducing a disciplined attention, and a bad beginning on this account may establish a backwardness which later may not be overcome without the individual attention that is impossible in the teaching of large classes."

Professor G. W. A. Luckey, of the University of Nebraska, listing the causes of retardation, puts at the foot of his list "bad inheritance, unredeemable defects, physical and mental," and at the very top, "ignorance and indifference on the part of parents." Most investigators would evaluate these contrasting causes in precisely the same way. The inference, needless to say, is that we need never hope to bring about an appreciable diminution in the number of retarded children until parents are more fully enlightened as to their duties and responsibilities. It is therefore good to find that a nation-wide campaign of enlightenment is well under way, together with an ever-increasing extension of agencies for the work of rescuing the retarded and fitting them to achieve success in the school and in the world.

Eight years ago there were in all the United States only three "clearing-houses for retarded children." These were the psychological clinic of the University of Pennsylvania, established by Professor Witmer in 1896; a civic psychological clinic, opened in 1909, in connection with the schools of Los Angeles; and the psychological clinic of Clark University, at Worcester, Massachusetts, established in the same year as a department of that university's splendid Children's Institute.

To-day, as part of the regular activities of universities and normal schools, there are psychological clinics in more than a dozen States, including California, Colorado, Connecticut, Iowa, Kansas, Louisiana, Massachusetts, Michigan, Minnesota, New York, Ohio, Pennsylvania, and Washington. At least four States—Indiana, Massachusetts, New York, and Pennsylvania—have psychological clinics in operation as adjuncts of hospitals. California, Illinois, Missouri, New York, and Pennsylvania have similar clinics in direct connection with the public school system. Ohio has one connected with a vocational-guidance bureau. And in some States—such as Connecticut, Illinois, and Massachusetts—psychological clinics are also in operation for the special purpose of aiding in the proper disposition of cases brought before the juvenile courts.

Even more rapid has been the development of ear, eye, throat, and dental clinics for the needs of school children. As an outgrowth, too, of the discoveries of the past few years, there has been a widespread movement in the direction of establishing special schools and classes in which the retarded may receive the care necessary to enable them to make up for lost time, or, when this is out of the question, to equip them for as happy and useful a life as is possible under their exceptional mental limitations. Unquestionably a splendid beginning has been made in the warfare against retardation—a beginning not surpassed by similar effort in any foreign land, and certain to prove of great value to the American nation.

But, if it is to prove of the utmost possible value, there must be active co-operation by the public generally and by parents in particular. Society must insist on every child being given hygienically decent surroundings, and parents in the mass must become increasingly alive to their responsibilities and opportunities in developing the mentality of their young. To reiterate:

It may be considered as definitely established to-day that the vast majority of cases of mental backwardness are the result, not of organic brain defects, not of true feeble-mindedness, but of remediable physical conditions or faulty training in the home.

It may be considered as established that even seemingly incurable cases will often yield to expert treatment.

And it may be considered as established that, of the cases which cannot be successfully handled, a large proportion are cases which could have been successfully handled had they been recognised and given expert treatment during early childhood.

Let every parent of a dull child act, and act promptly, to ascertain from some expert just why his child is dull, and what can and should be done to overcome the dullness. Let every parent of every child make it his business to learn and heed the laws of physical and mental hygiene as applicable to his child, with a view to insuring that the child shall not be afflicted with preventable mental backwardness. This is one of the prime duties of parenthood.

CHAPTER II

THE ONLY CHILD

FIFTEEN years ago a boy was born of prosperous New York parents. His arrival was exceptionally welcome, for his father and mother had been living in dread that theirs might prove a childless marriage. They had fervently promised themselves that if their fondest hopes were realised and a child granted to them, nothing that loving devotion could accomplish would be left undone to secure for the little one the best possible start in life. As a first step in the fulfilment of this promise, they decided soon after their son's birth to remove from New York to a pleasant residential suburb, where fresh air abounded, and where the adverse environmental influences of the crowded city streets were utterly unknown.

Seemingly, no decision could have been wiser; seemingly, no child could have been brought up amid more favourable surroundings than their boy enjoyed in the splendid home they provided for him on a beautiful slope crested with pines. Yet, despite all the love lavished on him, despite the prodigious efforts to keep him well and strong, he did not thrive.

Before he was seven he displayed "nervous" symptoms that threw his parents into a panic. He suffered from "night terrors," he became excitable and irritable. The eminent physician to whom he was taken made the flattering diagnosis that the only trouble with the boy was an unusually sensitive nervous organisation; prescribed sedatives, advised outdoor exercise, warned against overstudy, and so forth. Unfortunately, he did not also emphasise the necessity for simplification of the child's environment as a preventive of nerve strain. Nor did he dwell on the supreme importance to physical, no less than moral, welfare of sedulously cultivating in the little fellow the virtues of courage, self-control, and self-denial. Perhaps he did not think it needful to speak of these things to such evidently well-bred and well-intentioned parents; perhaps he did not think of these things at all.

In any event, while acting on his advice as to stimulating animal activity and retarding brain function, the father and mother continued to minister to their son's every whim, and eternally busied themselves devising amusements and distractions for him. In time the "night terrors" were no longer in evidence; but the excitability and irritability persisted, and presently other unpleasant traits appeared, notably a tendency to conceit and selfishness. Naturally, this did not make the poor youngster any too popular among the few playmates with whom his parents allowed him to associate, and naturally the parents blamed the playmates for not appreciating the "sensitiveness" of his disposition. Thus matters continued until his twelfth year, when his father suddenly awoke to the fact that, intellectually, the naughty playmates were considerably ahead of the good little boy. For the first time common sense scored a distinct triumph over excessive and indiscreet parental love; the governess who had been unable to handle her self-willed pupil was dismissed, and the boy was sent to school.

There he has been painfully gaining the discipline—the lessons in self-mastery—that should have been given him in the nursery. But he still is lamentably arrogant and selfish; he still finds it difficult to get along with other boys. Whether his schoolmates will take the trouble to help him overcome the handicap of his early rearing is questionable; and however this may be, it is hardly likely that the character defects unnecessarily acquired during his childhood will be wholly rooted out.

It must regretfully be added that this boy's case is not an exceptional one. Rather, it is typical of the plight of most "only children," who, no matter what their advantages of birth, too often reach manhood and womanhood sadly handicapped and markedly inferior to other children. In a vague way, to be sure, parents with only one child have long realised that they are confronted with special problems in child training; but there is abundant proof that in innumerable instances they signally fail to grasp these problems clearly and work them out satisfactorily.

Everyday observation supports this statement, and it is confirmed by the findings of modern medical, psychological, and sociological investigation. Statistically, its most important corroboration is forthcoming from the results of a census of "only children," undertaken some years ago by the psychological department of Clark University in consequence of certain suggestive indications noticed in the responses received to a *questionnaire* on peculiar and exceptional children.

Of the thousand children described in these responses it was observed that forty-six were specifically mentioned as being "only children," although none of the queries in the *questionnaire* asked directly or indirectly about such children. The presumption was that a number of the remaining children described in the responses were also of the only-child class. But even if such were not the case, the total of forty-six was surprisingly high, since, according to reliable vital statistics, the average progeny of fertile marriages is six, with an only-child average of one out of every thirteen fertile marriages; that is, a proportion of one only child to every seventy-eight children, as contrasted with the proportion of one in fewer than every twenty-two of the "peculiar" children described in the *questionnaire* reports.

Moreover, on dividing these reports into three groups based on the "advantageous," "neutral," and "disadvantageous" character of the peculiarities mentioned, it was found that while considerably less than half of the total number of children fell into the disadvantageous group, two-thirds of the "only children" had to be put into it. Naturally this suggested the desirability of a special investigation with reference to the only child, and accordingly a second *questionnaire* was issued, with queries relating to age, sex, nationality, health, amusements, intellectual ability, moral traits, and so forth. In this way, from school teachers and other disinterested observers, definite information was obtained concerning nearly four hundred "only children"—information which, as finally tabulated and analysed by the director of the investigation, Doctor E. W. Bohannon, is of great significance to the parents of every only child and to all interested in individual and racial improvement.

The age average of those whose ages were given—nearly three hundred—was twelve years, including about sixty ranging in age from seventeen to thirty-five. About four-fifths were of American parentage, while the proportion with regard to sex was, roughly speaking, one-third male and two-thirds female, a disparity doubtless attributable in part to the circumstances of the investigation. About one hundred were said not to be in good health, and another hundred to be in outright bad health. In one hundred and thirty-three out of two hundred and fifty-eight cases the temperament was described as "nervous." Precocity was another often-mentioned trait; but on the average the beginning of school life was from a year and a half to two years later than is usual, and in the performance of school work the *questionnaire* responses also revealed a marked inferiority on the part of many "only children."

In their social relations only eighty were reported as "normal," while one hundred and thirty-four out of a total of two hundred and sixty-nine got along badly with other children, usually because they were unwilling or did not know how to make concessions, or were stubbornly set on having their own way. On this important point Doctor Bohannon says, in detail:

"When they disagree with other children it is usually because of a desire to rule. If they fail in this desire they are likely to refuse to associate with the children who cause the failure, and in a measure succeed in the wish to have their own way, either by choosing younger companions whom they can control, or older ones who are willing to indulge them. Many do not care for a large number of companions, and select one or two for friends, with whom they prefer to spend most of their time. . . . In numerous instances . . . a marked preference for the company of older people is manifest, even when opportunity for younger company is present. But this is no doubt due less to a dislike of suitable companionship than to their inability to understand and be understood by children of near their own age. It is plainly evident that they have as deep longings for society as the children of other families, but their isolated home life has failed to give them equal skill and ability in social matters. They do not so well understand how to make approaches, to concede this thing and that."

Of two hundred and forty-five in attendance at school, more than one hundred "only children" were recorded as not being normally interested in active games, sixty-two of these scarcely playing at all. "If left to their own devices," Doctor Bohannon infers from the reports which he received concerning the inactive sixty-two, "they are pretty sure to be found in the schoolroom with their teachers at intermission. A number of the boys prefer to play with the girls at strictly girls' games, such as keeping house with dolls, and generally come to be called girl-boys."

Effeminacy, in fact, is an unpleasantly frequent characteristic of the male only child, and was noted in case after case described in the replies to the *questionnaire*. Selfishness was set down as the dominant trait in ninety-four "only children" of both sexes, and many others were described as being unusually bad-tempered, vain, naughty, or untruthful.[3]

These depressing findings have since been confirmed by other investigators, some of whom have contributed specially to our knowledge of the state of the only child in adult life. For instance, the well-known English psychologist, Havelock Ellis, studying the life histories of four hundred eminent men and women, found the low percentage of 6.9 for "only children," indicating unmistakably the persistence of the intellectual inferiority brought out by the answers to the Bohannon *questionnaire*. There would also seem to be no doubt that egotism and social inadaptability characterise, the adult only child no less than the immature one.

"In later life," affirms the American psychopathologist, A. A. Brill, who has made a special study of the only child from both a medical and psychological point of view, "he is extremely conceited, jealous, and envious. He begrudges the happiness of friends and acquaintances, and he is therefore shunned and disliked." Besides which, speaking from wide experience as a practising specialist in New York City, Doctor Brill insists that the only child, at any age of life, is peculiarly liable to fall a victim to hysteria, neurasthenia, and other serious functional nervous and mental maladies; and his belief, as I happen to know from their personal statements to me, is shared by other observant neurologists and psychopathologists, such as Doctors James J. Putnam and I. H. Coriat, of Boston.

This is a point of special interest, for the reason that recent medical research has made it certain that the maladies in question are one and all rooted in faulty habits of thought, usually resultant from errors of training in childhood. Chief among these errors, according to all modern neurologists, is an upbringing which tends to develop excessive occupation with thoughts of self. But this is precisely the kind of upbringing given the majority of "only children." Here again the Bohannon investigation affords impressive evidence. One of the queries included in the *questionnaire* bore on the treatment accorded the only child when at home, and it is indeed significant that in about 75 per cent. of the replies received it was stated that the policy of the parents was one of extreme indulgence.

"Had her own way in everything," "Her parents gratify her every whim," "She is surrounded by adults who indulge her too much," "Humoured," "Petted," "Coddled," are some of the expressions frequently employed to describe the parental treatment. Many of the answers sent to Doctor Bohannon also testify to an over-anxiety with respect to the child's welfare that might easily give rise to undue feelings of self-importance or to an unhealthy habit of introspection. "His mother was always unduly anxious about him when he was out of her sight," "She is thought to be quite delicate, and great care is taken of her; she is kept in a warm room and seldom allowed to go out," "His home treatment has made a baby of him," may fairly be cited as typical statements returned by Doctor Bohannon's respondents.

[3] Doctor Bohannon's report ought to be carefully read by the parents of every "only child." It is published in *The Pedagogical Seminary*, vol. v, p. 475 *et seq.*

Is it any wonder that the average only child grows up deficient in initiative and self-reliance? Is it any wonder that, under the stress of some sudden shock, he reacts badly, allowing himself to be overwhelmed by it, even to the extent of perhaps becoming a neurasthenic wreck? In short, can it be doubted that the handicap under which he too often has to struggle painfully through life is not a handicap imposed by Nature but is solely of his parents' making?

Sometimes this is all too clearly appreciated in later life by the child himself, and the parental error is bitterly resented; or, if the sense of filial piety be sufficiently strong, is splendidly excused. As in this fragment from an autobiographical statement by an only child:

"Of the selfishness of which a frank woman accused me, my parents were, up to that time, quite as unconscious as I. She had asked my mother to drive with her to the home of a friend in a neighbouring town, where the two were invited to spend the night. My mother declined, on the ground that I, at that time about nine, could not comb my hair and pin my collar properly for school in the morning; and as we then had no maid and my father could at best only have buttoned my frock, the objection seemed insurmountable. But the family friend called me by the ugly title of naughty, selfish little girl, and chided mother for allowing me to monopolise her time, contending that she was making me selfish and dependent.

"Perhaps she was. But I protest that it could hardly have been otherwise, considering that she had in full measure the world-old desire of mothers to spend themselves for their children, and only one child to spend herself on. It had not occurred to my mother, I am confident, that her habit of ministering to me constantly was pampering; nor had I, in going to her for services that I might easily have learned to perform for myself, made demands in the manner of the arrogant spoiled child."[4]

The compelling power of mother-love and father-love must, of a truth, be recognised in extenuation of the spoiling of the only child. But the fact of the spoiling remains, and the fact also that when the spoiling is achieved the parental pride and joy will be turned to grief and bitter lamentation. The pity of it is that the only child, simply because he is the only child, ought to be able to grow up healthier, wiser, and more efficient than other children.

For, as psychologists are insisting more and more emphatically, the health, happiness, and efficiency of adult life depend preponderantly on the home influences of early childhood; and, obviously, in a home where the parental attention can be concentrated on a single child, better results should be attained than when the work of training involves a division of the attention among several children. Unhappily, when it is a question of training an only child, too many parents seem to take it for granted that training is entirely unnecessary, that their child is innately so good that he will develop of his own accord into one of the best of men.

In reality, as modern psychology has made very clear, every child at the outset of his life is much like every other child, a plastic, unmoral little creature, exceedingly impulsive and exceedingly receptive, readily impressed for good or evil

[4] *Everybody's Magazine,* vol. xv, p. 693.

by the influences that surround him. Childhood, to repeat a truism hackneyed to psychologists, but seemingly unappreciated by most people, is pre-eminently the suggestible period of life. It is then, when the critical faculty still is undeveloped, that whatever ideas are presented to the mind are most surely absorbed by it, to sink into its subconscious depths, and there form the nucleus for whole systems of thought afterward manifesting as habits. Herein lurks the special peril to the only child afflicted with over-loving, over-anxious parents.

Their perpetual solicitude for him, acting as a suggestion of irresistible force, tends to engender in him a mental attitude out of which may afterward spring, according to the subsequent circumstances of his life, a cold, heartless, calculating selfishness, or a morbid self-anxiety, perhaps eventuating in all sorts of neurotic symptoms. If, as a boy, he is too closely and constantly associated with his mother, the force of suggestion again, acting largely through the imitative instinct, may lead to a development of those feminine traits frequently characteristic of male only children, and often involving pathological conditions of dire social as well as individual significance. Further still, by restricting unduly the intercourse of only children with playmates of their own age, as is often done, one of the finest agencies in development through the power of suggestion is left unutilised. There is a world of truth in the lament of the only child from whose autobiography I have already quoted:

"All this carefulness kept me uncontaminated by the naughtiness of little street Arabs, but it also limited my opportunity to imitate where imitation is easiest—among those of my own age; it stunted the initiativeness and inventiveness that might, in normal conditions, have developed in me; and it left me lacking in adaptability. I sometimes disloyally wonder if my chances of being a tolerable citizen might not have been as good if I had been permitted to 'run wild,' and thus secure for myself the companionship I could not have at home."

Of course, association with other children means at least an occasional hard knock, and hard knocks are, above all else, what the doting mother wishes to avoid for her darling boy. She forgets that they are certain to be experienced, soon or late, and that the earlier her boy is fitted to withstand them the better they will be withstood. She forgets, too, that if the suggestions emanating from playmates are not invariably suggestions for good, they may easily be counteracted, without sacrificing the advantages to be gained from association with playmates, by proper training in the quiet of the home.

Always, let me repeat, it is the home training that counts for most. If the only child turns out well, the credit must go to the parents; if, alas! he turns out badly, if he becomes a monster of selfishness or a neurotic weakling, the blame must likewise be theirs.

And now it becomes necessary to add that, if in less degree, the "favourite child" in a family is exposed to dangers similar to those menacing the unwisely brought up "only child." That parent of several children is making a sad mistake if he singles out any one of his children for special affection and solicitude. The consequences of such favouritism are twofold, affecting adversely, perhaps disastrously, both the child unduly favoured and the child or children comparatively slighted. So far as the former is concerned, the outcome, when the favouritism involves really excessive love and anxiety, is pretty sure to be much like that in the case of the average only child. That is to say, there is always more than a possibility that the favourite child, no matter how good his inherited qualities, will grow up arrogant, self-centred, and neurotic.

He is usually in less danger than the only child of growing up deficient in initiative and social adaptability. For, unless his parents constantly interfere in his behalf, daily intercourse with his brothers and sisters is bound to impress on him at an early age the necessity for developing self-reliance and for making concessions to the rights and susceptibilities of others. On the other hand, because he is the favourite child and because his brothers and sisters instinctively resent this, his intercourse with them is likely to be attended with more than the usual amount of friction. Thereby an additional stress will be put on a nervous system already more or less strained by the fussing and fretting of indulgent, unthinking parents. During childhood, it is true, he may not give marked evidence of neural enfeeblement. But, soon or late, if a kindly fortune does not rescue him at an early age from the harmful home environment—as, for example, by his removal to a good boarding-school—one may count on his displaying striking eccentricities of character and conduct, if not positively pathological conditions.

Consequently, his whole prospects for adult life will be adversely affected. The selfishness fostered by his father's, or mother's, excessive devotion may become intensified rather than lessened by friction with envious brothers and sisters, with the result that the favourite child passes into manhood abnormally deficient in altruistic qualities, and even abnormally misanthropic. "A favourite son, a bachelor of sixty-two years, who was a wealthy retired merchant," notes the psychopathologist Brill, "told me that whenever there was a rise in the market he suffered from severe depression and fits of envy, simply because he knew that some of his friends would make money. He himself had no interest in the market." And, speaking as an observer who has closely studied the subject, Doctor Brill unhesitatingly adds that, like so many "only children," almost all favourite children are in later years "selfish, unhappy, and morose."

It is true there are notable exceptions. Some favourite children are brought up so well that, aside perhaps from a tendency to nervous ailments, they display no peculiarities and pass through life creditably, possibly brilliantly. But such exceptions are conspicuous by their rarity, for the excellent reason that parents who are wise enough to rear favourite children well are commonly wise enough not to show favouritism to any of their children.

For, no matter, how much the favourite child may benefit from the extra care bestowed on him, the mere fact that he is thus selected for special attention is sure to work to the detriment of the other children in the family. When, as often happens, there is only one other child, the effect on that child may be catastrophic. When the favourite child has several brothers and sisters there is less danger that any of these will be really disastrously affected. At best, however, they will chafe under the injustice of the favouritism shown by the parent or parents; and, besides instinctively drawing together for mutual consolation and defence, they may develop a spirit of rebellion destructive to the peace and well-being of the entire family.

CHAPTER III

THE CHILD WHO SULKS

NOBODY likes a chronically sulky child. Even his own parents are apt to lose patience with him. In common with outsiders, though in less degree, they regard his sulkiness as indicative of an unpleasant disposition, calling for stern disciplinary measures. Seldom do they see it for what it really is—the result of conditions for which the child is not to blame, and a danger-signal giving warning that unless a successful effort is made to ascertain and correct the sulk-producing conditions, the child will enter adult life under a tremendous handicap.

As I write, there comes before my mind's eye the weary face and form of an old acquaintance, with whose life history I am familiar. This man, though not yet in his forties, and with health unbroken by any serious disease, is nevertheless one of the unemployable. He is willing enough to work, he affirms, and in his time has had many positions. But he has been able to hold none of these. There has always developed friction between him and his employer or between him and fellow-employees. For a few days, perhaps a few weeks, after gaining a new position, things go smoothly with him. He is confident, even enthusiastic. Then, for no apparent reasons, he acquires a "grouch." He conceives the idea that his "job" is not sufficiently remunerative, or that he is not being treated with due respect. Sometimes he gives vent to his feelings in words that promptly effect his dismissal. More often, giving no explanation, he sullenly stops work of his own accord.

Yet he began life with seemingly excellent prospects. His parents were well to do and could give him every educational advantage. And in early childhood he was both a bright boy and a well-behaved boy. A little later, when he began to go to school, there was a noticeable change in his disposition. His parents learned that he did not associate with other boys as readily as might be desired. They noticed that he developed a tendency to keep much by himself, to be uncommunicative, to smile seldom—in fine, to sulk. But, though they noticed this, they fancied it was only a passing phase which he would in time outgrow. They failed to take his sulkiness seriously—failed, that is to say, to recognise in it a sign that something was amiss which should be seriously investigated. To-day, perhaps wholly because no investigation was made and no corrective treatment attempted, this unfortunate man is finding life a heavy burden.

With all the emphasis at my command I would say, When a child frequently sulks, it is *always* a sure indication of mental or nervous stress. If parents have a child who is sulky, they should neither ignore the sulkiness nor accuse him of wilful naughtiness and try to improve him by scoldings and punishments. They should recognise, in his habit of sulking, evidence of one of two things: either that they are not bringing him up as they should, or that he is suffering from some unsuspected physical disability, of which his sullen, morose, peevish disposition is symptomatic. It may be that this disability is an irremediable one, such as organic weakness of the brain. But the chances are that it is caused by functional disturbances easily discovered and easily cured. The parent is neglecting his full duty to his child if he fail to inquire into the child's physical condition.

One of the commonest causes of sulkiness is nothing more or less than indigestion. Everybody knows that if a baby's food disagrees with him the baby is pretty sure to be fretful and irritable. But parents too often forget that, in the case of older children, mental and moral eccentricities may be traced to the same cause. When food is not properly digested, there is an impoverishing and poisoning of the blood. This means that the brain is poorly nourished, and a poorly nourished brain means a general weakening of the power to think and to will. It means, too, a heightening of nervous irritability, coupled with a tendency to take a gloomy view of life. Under these circumstances, it is not at all surprising to find sulkiness becoming characteristic of a child of any age, as in a typical case reported by Doctor T. A. Williams, of Washington, a specialist in the treatment of the nervous diseases of children.

Doctor Williams' patient was a ten-year-old girl, the daughter of a clergyman. She had been lovingly reared, and until the age of nine had been easy to manage, vivacious, and happy. Then there came a marked change in her behaviour. She became easily irritated, had frequent crying spells, and frequent fits of sulkiness. Besides this, she had difficulty in studying. Thinking that she had been overworking, her parents took her out of school, although her mother noticed that she was less inclined to sulk when kept busy.

What Doctor Williams found, after a long and careful examination of the girl and questioning of her parents, was unmistakable evidence of nerve deficiency, due chiefly to faulty diet, and aggravated by "parental interference, well meant, but entirely injudicious." She had been eating oatmeal and meat to excess, had been taking her principal meal at night, and had gone to bed soon after it. Doctor Williams ordered that her allowance of meat and oatmeal be cut down, that she eat her principal meal at noon, and that she stay up for at least an hour after her evening meal. Further, he gave these directions:

"On waking in the morning, the child must make a practice of getting up at once, instead of ruminating in bed. Parents must avoid criticising her about trifles, and her behaviour must be left to take care of itself at present. Her affections should be indulged and reciprocated. She must be given plenty to do and sent back to school in a few days."

Under this treatment the girl's disposition began immediately to improve. Within two weeks her mother reported to Doctor Williams that she was as "happy and joyous" as she had formerly been. No longer was her stomach being loaded with food it could not digest; and with the removal of this source of toxic irritation, together with the suggested changes in her parents' handling of her, she had become a different child.

On the other hand, underfeeding may be, and often is, a cause of sulkiness, owing to the inadequate nourishment the underfed child's brain receives and the general weakness of his system. Sulkiness, again, may be associated with an insufficiency of physical exercise, or with failure to make sure that the child's living and sleeping quarters are properly ventilated. Fresh air is as essential as digestible food to the maintenance of nervous balance. When, as sometimes happens, children are obliged to spend their school hours in dusty, ill-ventilated classrooms, when they return to homes with few windows, and these seldom open, and when they sleep in a tainted, vitiated atmosphere, it is indeed hard for them to see life in bright colours. Besides which, to prevent or cure sulkiness in a child, it is not enough to keep school and home well ventilated, and let the child play outdoors as much as possible. It is necessary also to see to it that the child is so conditioned that he will have no difficulty in adequately breathing the fresh outdoor air.

To a physician in a Western city there was brought a boy, nine years old, with a face so flat, expressionless, and frog-like, that persons who knew him thought he was feeble-minded. His school teacher reported that his mind seemed a blank and that he was also hard of hearing. His parents complained that he was selfish and sullen. The boy seemed doomed to a life of misery.

But, making a physical examination of him, the doctor found reason to think otherwise. He discovered no real brain defect. In the cavity back of the boy's nose he found an abnormal growth of adenoid-tissue that of itself might account for the boy's stupidity and sulky disposition, as well as for his deafness. The diseased tissue acted as an irritant and a drag on his nervous energy; and, in addition, by interfering with the intake of oxygen it lowered the nutrition of the brain.

The adenoid growth was removed. Gradually the appearance of the unfortunate boy's face changed for the better. His hearing improved. He began to take an interest in school work, and studied to real advantage. Consideration for others took the place of his habitual selfishness, and he sulked no more.

Adenoids, dullness, deafness, and sullenness often are intimately associated. The parents of a sulky child will therefore do well to ascertain whether adenoid trouble is present. Its presence is usually plainly indicated by the flat, insipid appearance of the victim's face and by his habit of breathing through his mouth, particularly when asleep. If there is any reason to suspect adenoids, parents should take their children to a competent physician without delay.

Further, and on general principles, they should have their children's teeth thoroughly examined by a good dentist. A child whose teeth are decayed is a child suffering both from nerve irritation and from some degree of poisoning, due to his swallowing food that has become infected by its contact with the germs of dental caries. Such a child has abundant reason to feel uncomfortable, pessimistic, and sullen. So has a child whose teeth, if not decayed, are crowded together.

Yet another common, and often unsuspected, physical cause of sulkiness in children is eye-strain. Most of us are under the impression that when a person is afflicted with eye-strain he is certain to have painful or, at least, unpleasant sensations in his eyes. This is by no means always the case. During childhood and youth there may be no telltale eye symptoms at all. But defective eyesight may give rise to various nervous conditions; sulkiness is one manifestation.

An eight-year-old girl, previously in good health, and with no more nervousness than is displayed by the average child, began to show traits that worried her parents. She became difficult to control, querulous, and sullen to an extent that bordered on melancholia. In addition, she complained of indigestion and headache, symptoms which caused her parents to take her to a physician for treatment. His medicines and the course of diet he prescribed did her no good, and another physician was consulted. Then began for this unfortunate little girl a weary round of examinations by doctor after doctor. Every means of curing her headaches and indigestion seemed unavailing, and her nervousness and sullenness increased apace. Finally, one physician, in spite of the fact that the girl's eyesight seemed normal, suggested that she be examined by an eye specialist. Then, for the first time, it was discovered that she had a serious ocular defect. According to Doctor Percy R. Wood, who reported the case for the benefit of the medical profession in general, within six months after she first put on spectacles the girl was entirely free from digestive disturbances, her head had ceased to ache, and her melancholy moroseness had given way to normal good nature.

Occasionally sulkiness results from some special form of nervous disease. It may be an initial symptom of that strange malady of childhood, chorea. A child affected with chorea is restless, uneasy, and weak in muscular control. Muscles of the face twitch, the child has difficulty in using his hands, and, in later stages of the disease, the arms and legs make random, involuntary movements. In addition, just before or about the time the muscular weakness begins, there are sometimes signs of mental disturbance, described as follows by an authority on nervous diseases:

"These symptoms consist of a slight loss of memory and inability of the patients to apply themselves to their studies as well and continuously as formerly. Children who were previously of an obedient and mild disposition become irritable, obstinate, and perverse. They become insubordinate, lose their love of play, and are not as affectionate as was their wont. These phenomena are naturally looked upon as indubitable evidences of wilfulness, and are punished accordingly, thus frequently precipitating and aggravating the course of the disease."

Happily, sulkiness, as an early symptom of chorea, or of other grave nervous and mental disorders, is of comparatively infrequent occurrence. The things the parents of a sulky child need more particularly to inquire into are the amount and character of the food the child eats, the state of his digestion, his habits of exercise, the ventilation of the rooms in which he spends most of his time, the condition of his nose, mouth, and teeth, and his ability to see and hear distinctly. But it must be admitted that any or all of these common physical causes of sulkiness may be present, and the afflicted child nevertheless contrive to get along without sulking. And, on the opposite, when a child thus afflicted does sulk, the correction of the physical trouble is not always followed by a cessation of the sulkiness. For, precisely as in the case of the child who remains mentally backward after the correction of bodily defects responsible for his backwardness, it may be that a habit of sulking has become established. What is much worse, it may also be that the sulky child has a home environment that makes sulking almost inevitable.

Here we come to the central fact in the whole problem of sulkiness, for, nine cases out of ten, it is the home environment—the training a child receives, the parents' attitude towards him—that is primarily responsible for his sulking. The healthiest child in the world will sulk if his parents surround him with a sulk-breeding environment. He will sulk because *it is child nature to react appropriately to the suggestions received from the environment.* Every psychologist will bear out this statement. It also finds confirmation in the everyday experiences of all observant persons who have an opportunity to study children. It is all very well to exhort a child to be cheerful, to speak of "developing his will-power." But if the child's home surroundings are such as to fill his mind with depressing, disturbing ideas, he is bound to be influenced in his behaviour by these ideas. Parents are prone to forget this. They blame the sulky child when, in all justice, they ought to blame themselves.

Recently a veteran New England school teacher, talking with me on this question of sulkiness, said:

"There are times when I am tempted to believe that the home influence is *everything,* and that conditions of physical ill health have virtually nothing to do with sulkiness. Of course, I know that in reality physical conditions have to be taken into account, but my experiences with sulky children have been such that now, whenever I find a sulky child, I ask myself the question, 'What is wrong in that child's home?' If I have opportunity to investigate, I invariably find that something is wrong.

"My pupils are girls, eight and nine years old. Among them last year was one bright, attractive-looking little girl, to whom I felt drawn when she first appeared in the class. But I soon discovered that she was a difficult child. She neglected her school work, did in a careless, indifferent manner whatever she was obliged to do, and sulked at slight provocation. She had been examined by the school physician, who gave her a clean bill of health. My suspicion deepened that the child was the victim of an unfavourable home influence, and one day I suggested this to the principal of the school.

"'I am sure you are wrong,' said he. 'I happen to know the family. They are first-rate people, in good circumstances.'

"A little later, after I had again spoken to him of the girl's misconduct and sullenness, he told me:

"'You were right and I was wrong. Outwardly, everything seemed well with that family. But I now find that the parents have for some time been on the verge of seeking a divorce. They are bitter against each other and dispute over the child, giving her contrary orders. The mother will tell her to do something, the father will tell her not to do it. No wonder she is sullen and hard to deal with. She is to be taken from them and put in a good home.'

"This is an extreme instance, I have no doubt. But it is in line with what I am observing all the time. Therefore, I insist that sulkiness in children is, as a rule, a sure sign of unwise training in the home."

Many parents, though wholly unappreciative of the fact, inspire sulkiness in their children by setting them an example of sulkiness. A striking instance has lately come under my personal observation, in the experience of a mother who is continually being annoyed by the whining, sulky ways of her four-year-old daughter. She scolds the girl, she spanks her, but all to no good. Not once does it seem to occur to the mother that possibly her own habit of sulking when things do not go right may be blamed for the sulkiness of her child. She is precisely the kind of woman to whom the learned Professor Paul Dubois addresses these scathing words:

"You, madam, who complain of the irritability of your little girl, could you not suppress your own?. . . Remember the proverb, 'The fruit does not fall far from the tree.'"

This factor of example in the causing of sulkiness is something that parents frequently ignore. In a general way they realise that their children are likely to imitate them, but they do not appreciate the subtle force which imitation exercises in forming the mental states and moral attitudes of the young. Time and again we see parents talking and acting as though children had no eyes or ears or memories; as though, indeed, they were beings quite insensitive to the sights and sounds of their surroundings.

Yet normal children are the most sensitive and the most "suggestible" of beings. Let father snarl and mother sulk, and little Johnny or Mary may be pretty confidently counted on to snarl and sulk likewise—unless by a happy chance Johnny and Mary have playmates or relatives whose lives radiate sufficiently strong suggestions of cheerfulness to offset the parents' unhappy influence. Instruction is much, but example is more. Or, as wise Pastor Witte puts it, "Instruction begins, example accomplishes."

But, if the parental example is good, if the child's physical condition is excellent, and if he nevertheless is a sulker—what then? Again, it must be insisted that the trouble rests with some fault in his upbringing, some error in the parental policy. If there is more than one child in the family, it may be that the sulkiness is a symptom of jealousy. The parents should ask themselves in all seriousness whether they have given this particular child any reason to sulk, by showing greater favour, or seeming to show greater favour, to his brothers and sisters. Or, possibly, the sulkiness is indicative, not of jealousy, but of a feeling of inferiority due to the child's fear that he is not quite so bright as other children. In that case the parents may be sure that in some way, however unwittingly, they have failed to bring into their child's life enough happiness and joy to prevent the feeling of inferiority from becoming dominant in his mind. Perhaps, for the matter of that, they have themselves been instrumental in forcing on the child recognition of his inferior mental status.

There are parents whose behaviour when dealing with a mentally retarded child is—often quite unconsciously—that of a censorious judge upbraiding a criminal. They nag, they harass, they urge the child to greater effort, never questioning that he can of his own accord improve his ability to learn. Perhaps he is mentally deficient, perhaps he is suffering from some remediable physical cause of retardation, perhaps the method by which he is being taught is not suited to his type of mind. To all these possibilities the parents do not give a moment's thought. The child is stupid; it must be his fault; he should be forced to mend his ways. So they pester the little unfortunate. And when to retardation he gradually adds sullenness, they are more incensed than before. But, in point of cold fact, whose is the fault? Not the child's, surely. Perpetual nagging is a first-class means of producing sulkiness in any child, whether he be mentally retarded, unusually bright, or just a plain "average" child.

Another almost equally efficacious means is untruthfulness on the part of parents in their relations with the child. There are some parents who think it not at all amiss to deceive their children. They make promises to them which they do not intend to keep. They threaten them with punishments that never materialise. They make untruthful replies to questions the children put to them. The children are not imbeciles. They note these broken promises, these empty threats, these untruthful replies. They lose faith in their parents, and sometimes it happens that their loss of faith manifests itself in a gloomy brooding, a sullen resentment against the parents. The parents, on their side, regard the sulky child as maliciously naughty and evil-minded. Not an inkling do they have of their own share in the making of the condition of which they complain. They blame only the child.

Even the practice, common among parents, of telling their children "white lies" with regard to delicate matters is at times productive of sulkiness *as a symptom of nervousness due to inner mental conflict*. Almost every child is at an early age inquisitive about his origin and the manner of his coming into the world. If his questions on these subjects are evaded or answered in a fantastic way, the child's curiosity is likely to be increased rather than satisfied. In exceptional cases there may result an obsessional pondering of the evaded topic, intensified when the child discovers that his parents have deceived him. Extreme nervousness, accompanied with sullenness, is then a likely result. But, apart altogether from the possibility that nervousness and sulkiness may be caused by parental deception of this sort, the danger of losing control over their children is itself serious enough to warn parents to be straightforward in answering their children's queries regarding sex subjects.

Havelock Ellis, the foremost authority on the psychology of sex, does not exaggerate when he assures us:

"Even if there were no other reasons against telling children fairy tales of sex instead of the real facts, there is one reason which ought to be decisive with every mother who values her influence over her child. He will very quickly discover, either by information from others or by his own natural intelligence, that the fairy tale that was told him in reply to a question about a simple matter of fact was a lie. With that discovery, his mother's influence over him in all such matters vanishes forever, for not only has a child a horror of being duped, but he is extremely sensitive about a rebuff of this kind, and never repeats what he has been made to feel was a mistake to be ashamed of. He will not trouble his mother with any more questions on this matter; he will not confide in her; he will himself learn the art of telling 'fairy tales' about sex matters. He had turned to his mother in trust, she had not responded with equal trust, and she must suffer the punishment, as Henriette Fürth puts it, of seeing 'the love and trust of her son stolen from her by the first boy he makes friends with in the street.'"[5]

Joy is a natural consequence of a child's affection for, and faith in, his parents. Resentfulness, bitterness, sullenness, are natural consequences of loss of affection and faith. The parents of a sullen child must always ask themselves if, through deception of any sort, they have forfeited the child's esteem for them. They must further ask themselves if, by intentional or unintentional unkindness of a persistent sort, they have embittered the child. They must also put to themselves the question: "Have I in some way erred so as to make my child sullen by the force of a bad example?" And, lastly, they must not forget to probe, through the aid of a skilled physician, for possible physical causes of mental and nervous stress.

If they do not adopt this course, if they allow the child to go on sulking, or if they increase his sulkiness by mishandling him, let me again warn them that they may be hopelessly limiting his chances for success and happiness in manhood. Character distortions of some sort are certain to result; even his bodily health itself may be affected. For, just as sulkiness often is a product of some physical disorder, so may it, in turn, become a *cause* of physical disorder. To sulk is essentially to be in a disturbed emotional state, and recent scientific research has established that such states, particularly if intense or long continued, have a highly unfavourable influence on the bodily organism. This has been most clearly shown in the case of anger and worry, the former of which always is, while the latter often is, basic in sulkiness.

All parents, indeed, ought to familiarise themselves with the physiology of anger and worry. Once really appreciative of the possible bodily effects of these emotional states, they would, on the one hand, be more careful to train their children early in emotional control, and, on the other, would be more chary about subjecting them to conditions involving emotional stress. Anger—and, equally, worry—is liable, for one thing, to derange profoundly the workings of the digestive organs. How profoundly it may derange them has recently been demonstrated conclusively by some remarkable scientific observations on animals and human beings.

A prime requisite to good digestion is a free flow of saliva and gastric juice when food is chewed. There must literally be a preparatory automatic "watering" of the mouth and stomach. Ordinarily, this begins as soon as food is taken into the mouth—if one is hungry, it begins at the mere sight of food. But it has been proved that, no matter how appetising the food, the digestive flow stops almost altogether under the influence of anger.

This was first demonstrated by a Russian physiologist, Pawlow, experiment-

[5] Further discussion of this important subject will be found in the chapter on "Night Terrors."

ing with dogs so conditioned that he could see into their throats and stomachs. When a dog was irritated—as by showing it a cat which it was prevented from attacking—the flow of saliva and gastric juice instantly stopped, and did not begin again for some time after the dog had been calmed. Even a slight degree of irritability in the animal was sufficient to stop gastric secretion.

The same result has been repeatedly recorded by other scientists experimenting with cats, rabbits, guinea pigs, children, and full-grown men and women. One observer, a medical man named Hornborg, had as a patient a small boy in whom disease had caused an external opening large enough to allow a view of the workings of the stomach. Doctor Hornborg found that if he gave this boy food, after first angering him, his eating of the food was not accompanied by a flow of the gastric juice, which ordinarily flowed promptly and freely.

And, besides stopping the secretory processes of the stomach, anger stops its muscular movements as well, and also the movements of almost all the alimentary tract. Hence, food eaten during or soon after an outburst of anger or petulance is not properly taken up by the alimentary canal for final digestion, absorption, and elimination. Which means, it need scarcely be pointed out, that every part of the body suffers in some degree through diminished nutrition. And certain specific discomforts are likely to be experienced—sour stomach, gastric pains, headache, and so forth.

Equally striking is the effect of anger on the liver. One most important function of the liver is to store glycogen, or "animal starch," which is a source of energy when liberated from the liver into the blood in the form of sugar. Under normal conditions, an exceedingly small amount of sugar—all the body requires—is liberated. The liberation of a greater amount is a waste; and, if long continued, its excessive liberation has a fatally weakening effect on the system, constituting the serious disease known as diabetes.

Now, as has lately been proved by an American investigator, Doctor W. B. Cannon, of Harvard University, anger, or strong emotional excitement of any sort, immediately causes the liver to liberate sugar in excess. Doctor Cannon found this to be true in the case of both animals and human beings. Almost always a man examined after he had been angry or excited showed clear indications in the liquids of his body of glycosuria, or excessive sugar. Here is Doctor Cannon's summary of one of his most interesting observations:

"C. H. Fiske and I examined twenty-five members of the Harvard University football squad immediately after the final and most exciting contest of 1913, and found sugar in twelve cases. Five of these positive cases were among substitutes not called upon to enter the game. The only excited spectator of the Harvard victory who was examined also had a marked glycosuria, which on the following day had disappeared."[6]

Further than this, on testing the blood of excited and angry animals and people, Doctor Cannon discovered that it held in excess another substance which, like sugar, is usually present in the circulation in exceedingly minute quantities.

[6] "The Bodily Effects of Pain, Hunger, Fear, and Rage," pp. 75-76.

This substance, called adrenin, has some extraordinary properties. It is secreted by two small glands back of the kidneys. If artificially extracted and injected into the blood of a human being in any appreciable amount, it instantly has the effect of creating a sharp rise in blood pressure, the blood vessels being constricted and the heart beat appreciably increased. It also alters the distribution of the blood, driving it from the abdomen to the head and limbs. And for the time being it enormously increases muscular power and abolishes all feeling of fatigue.

Exactly similar effects, scientific research has proved, are brought about by the quantity of adrenin set free in the blood during periods of anger or other emotional stress. That is to say, not only does anger temporarily stop stomach action and abnormally stimulate the sugar-releasing function of the liver: it also imposes an unusual strain on the heart and the blood vessels.

Likewise with worry. It affects the heart, blood vessels, liver, and digestive organs as anger does. Even in the lower animals, and when occurring in comparatively slight degree, worry puts a stop to stomach movements and digestive secretions. Thus, in discussing with me the physiology of worry, Doctor Cannon stated:

"To give a significant illustration of how worry affects animals, as well as people, I might mention the case of a young male cat, the movements of whose stomach I studied by the aid of the Röntgen rays.

"For observation purposes, it was necessary to attach the cat to a holder. He made no resistance when this was done, but kept up a slight twitching of his tail from side to side, indicating that he was at least somewhat anxious as to what was going to happen to him.

"For more than an hour I watched his stomach by means of the rays, and during that time there was not the slightest beginning of peristaltic activity, the waves of muscular contraction being entirely absent.

"In another instance, that of a female cat with kittens, something happened to create an anxious mood while the cat was attached to the holder. Until that moment the cat had been contented, and the work of digestion was proceeding normally. But now the movements of the stomach entirely ceased, and the gastric wall became relaxed. Only after the cat had been petted and began to purr did the stomach movements start again.

"I have observed the same thing in dogs and guinea pigs. A very slight emotional disturbance is enough to affect their digestion unfavourably."

Affecting specifically the brain, heart, arteries, stomach, intestines, liver, and glands of internal secretion, worry also has a general adverse effect on the nervous system.

This adverse effect is unmistakably expressed by the haggard, drawn, gaunt aspect of the man who habitually worries, and by his persistent sensations of fatigue. What has happened is that his nerve cells are being deprived of the nutrition they need in order to energise him properly. When, on the contrary, the worrier succeeds in changing his mental state—when he contrives to look at things confidently and contentedly—then, in the words of Professor George Van Ness Dearborn, there is a resultant and most beneficial increase in "the operative enthusiasm of the nervous system and of its affectors, the muscles and the glands."

The moral to parents is obvious. Keep children as joyous and happy as possible. By instruction and example, start them early in the path of emotional control. Protect them from needless causes of fear, worry, and anger. And make special efforts to prevent the development or continuance of that curious and most injurious mental attitude—the attitude of sulkiness—grounded in anger and frequently grounded also in sentiments of worry, envy, hatred, and even despair.

CHAPTER IV

JEALOUSY

IN the preceding chapter reference was made to jealousy as a cause of sulkiness in children. Jealousy is itself a woeful handicap of childhood, and may be followed by disastrous consequences of many kinds. It has even been known to prompt children to acts as tragic as any committed by jealousy-driven adults. To cite a single instance:

In a small country town there lived a family of three persons—father, mother, and young son. Comfortably circumstanced, the parents testified their affection for their only child by loving care and gifts innumerable. Their great aim in life seemed to be to bring joy and pleasure into his life. The boy, for his part, reciprocated their love, and, though of a somewhat nervous temperament, was bright, vivacious, and amiable. There was nothing to mar the happiness of the family circle, which, to the delight of both parents, was one day enlarged by the addition of a little daughter.

They had taken it for granted that the coming of this baby sister would be equally pleasing to their boy, then nearly twelve years old. But his attitude towards her was indifferent, even cold; and, as time passed, he showed a dislike for the child as inexplicable as it was disappointing to his father and mother. Also, his disposition gradually changed. He was no longer high-spirited, but became moody and depressed. He would sit by himself for hours, lost in mournful reverie. His parents, rightly suspecting that something was preying on his mind, tried to get his confidence. He put them off with evasive answers, or brusquely asserted that he was "all right."

The true explanation came to them in startling and gruesome fashion. Late one afternoon, his father being absent from the house and his mother occupied downstairs, the boy made his way to the room, where his tiny sister was peacefully asleep in her crib. Only a short time passed before his mother's return upstairs, but in the interval the little one had been smothered to death by her jealous brother.

Such an instance of juvenile crime incited by the demon of jealousy is fortunately rare. But it by no means stands alone, and while the hand of reason usually restrains even jealous children, in no individual case is it possible to say with assurance that tragedy will not result if jealousy gets firm lodgment in the child's mind. If for this reason only, parents should regard with concern any repeated manifestations of jealousy, in no matter how mild and seemingly harmless a form. As a matter of fact, however, many parents are not in the least disturbed when their children give evidence of being jealous. Some parents seem to be positively pleased at signs of jealousy in their children, interpreting them as proofs of the ardour of the children's love. One thoughtless mother put it thus:

"My little Jack is so fond of me that he cannot bear to see me show attention to any other child. It is really amusing how displeased he gets. He will push the other child away, climb into my lap, and almost smother me with kisses. If I persist in paying attention to somebody else, he will pout in the cutest way until I take him in my arms again."

It may, to be sure, be difficult at times to refrain from smiling at the absurd behaviour of jealous children. Just the same, jealousy is never a smiling matter and is always something which parents should try to root out without delay. The jealous child, if uncorrected, is all too likely to grow into a jealous adult, with tendencies which bring misery to himself, and which, if it becomes a question of sex jealousy, may bring death to others. The parent who fails to attack jealousy when it first shows itself need not be surprised at any distortion of character or vagary of conduct that appears in later life. Jealousy, indeed, may have strange and startling physical consequences. Here, for example, is a story from the experience of a veteran physician:

"I was once summoned to visit a lady who was represented as being very ill. On my arrival I was shown to the so-called sick-room, where three persons were present—an old lady, her daughter, and the daughter's husband. All of them seemed in good health. When I inquired which was my patient, there was silence for a moment. Then the daughter said:

"'I am the patient, and my complaint is jealousy. I am jealous of my husband, and if you do not give me something to relieve me I shall go out of my mind.'

"This, on the face of it, seemed preposterous. She was a tall, fair, beautiful woman of about thirty. The husband, on the contrary, was several years older, a short, swarthy, plain man. It seemed to me more reasonable to suppose that he might have cause to be jealous of his wife, rather than she of him. But she persisted in her statement, and declared that she had good reason to feel jealous.

"The husband insisted he had done nothing to justify her jealousy. She reasserted he had. In the midst of an outburst, distressing to listen to, she fell into a queer fit. With rhythmic regularity, she went through various spasmodic convulsions. At one moment she would stand at full length, her body arched forward. The next instant she was in a sitting position, with her legs drawn up, her hands clutching her throat, and a guttural noise coming from her mouth. Then she would wildly throw her arms and legs around; after which she would rise to go through the same performance.

"It was necessary to give her a drug to quiet her. I learned that she had been subject to these attacks ever since she began to feel jealous of her husband. Inquiring more closely, I found that, quite without reason, she was specifically jealous of him in connection with a certain woman in the small town where he carried on his business. Thereupon I advised him, for the sake of her health and his own peace of mind, to remove to another town. This having been done, her jealousy abated and the convulsive seizures ceased."

Of course, this mode of treatment—if treatment it should be called—gave no guarantee that the jealousy and the consequent convulsions would not recur under other circumstances. What the jealous wife really needed was psychical re-education to give her a saner philosophy of life, enabling her to get a better grip on her emotions, and, through this, to control better the workings of her nervous system. Here we touch on what is far and away the most important fact in the problem of jealousy—a fact unappreciated by too many parents, and, for that matter, likewise unappreciated by most writers on the pedagogy of childhood.

This fact is that jealousy, being always an evidence of uncontrollable emotionality, and itself serving still further to weaken emotional control, may, and often does, give rise to functional mental and nervous troubles. These may appear during childhood, or their appearance may be postponed until adult life, as in the instance cited above. In either event, their underlying cause is always the same: failure to train the individual during early life to react with calmness, courage, and moderation to the stresses of existence.

In the case of a person of naturally phlegmatic nervous constitution, lack of such training does not do so much harm, for the reason that excessive emotional reactions are unlikely to occur, no matter what the provocation. But when there is any marked degree of sensitiveness in the nervous organisation—as there usually is in our land: Americans being conspicuously of the so-called nervous temperament—the need for training in emotional control becomes imperative. In the case of persons who have inherited any tendency to nervous ailments, persons burdened with what is technically known as a neuropathic diathesis, absence of this training may be disastrous.

Parents, accordingly, will make no mistake in regarding any persistent manifestation of jealousy in their children as—like sulkiness—a danger-signal of real urgency and as indicating a special need for careful upbringing. Also, they should not be surprised if jealousy begins to show itself at an extremely early age. Some instances are on record of its appearance before the end of the first year. The naturalist Darwin noted its presence in his son at the age of fifteen and a half months. Arnold L. Gesell, one of the few scientists to make any extended research of jealousy, found that "infants will variously hold out their arms, fret, whine, or burst into violent crying, cover their face with their hands, or sulk, when their mothers caress or hold another baby." From the end of the second year jealousy is much in evidence, and is most variously motivated.

Commonest of all, perhaps, is the jealousy occasioned by the advent of a little brother or sister, who is looked upon as a rival for the parents' affections. Or jealousy may be felt against one of the parents, little boys being frequently jealous of their fathers, and little girls of their mothers. Seemingly, they are unable to tolerate the love their parents feel for each other and would monopolise the affection of the parent of whom they are fonder. Again, there may be jealousy, sometimes of a violent sort, with regard to material possessions. Greatly to the profit of toy-makers, innumerable children have broken their toys to pieces in jealous rage at another child having been allowed to play with them. So, too, there may be jealousy with regard to food. A child will often eat food of which he is not really desirous, rather than see another gain pleasure from it.

As the child grows older, other objects and situations cause in him the unpleasant reaction of jealousy. On this point—the shifting causes of jealousy, through later childhood into adolescence—I cannot do better than quote at some length the findings of Professor M. V. O'Shea, of the University of Wisconsin, as given in his "Social Development and Education," a book of great value to parents and teachers:

"The jealous attitude is manifested most strikingly in children from the fifth year on, in situations where competitors seek to exalt themselves in the eyes of those who have favours to distribute, or where the deeds and virtues of rivals are extolled by outsiders. Let K. begin to describe in the family circle some courageous or faithful deed he has performed, or painful experience he has endured, or duties he has discharged, and C., his natural rival, will at once seek to minimise the importance of the particular act for which praise is sought, so that K. may not be too highly thought of. Then C. will endeavour to attract attention to his own worth by describing more meritorious deeds which he has himself performed. He cannot easily submit to the attempts of his rival to gain the admiration of the company before whom he wishes to exhibit himself. But it is different in situations where K. and C. are united in their interests, in opposition to other groups. Then C. is glad to reinforce the testimony of K. regarding his valorous deeds; and the principle works in just the same way when C. is seeking for favour, and K. is the jealous witness or the faithful comrade.

"It must be impressed that jealousy is an attitude assumed only by individuals in those situations in which they are competing for the same favours. Two children may be intensely jealous in their own homes; but they may abandon this attitude absolutely when they go into the world and compete as a unit with other groups. Normally, the jealousies between members of a family tend to disappear in the measure that their interests broaden, and they form new connections in the world. That is to say, according as persons cease to be keen rivals, they tend either to become indifferent to the successes of one another, or they may even rejoice in the good fortune of each other, and lose no opportunity to celebrate one another's virtues and merits. This latter stage is not reached, however, until rivalry, and so conflict, wholly ceases, and the contestants come to appreciate that their interests are mutual, and each can help himself best by extolling the other. This is frequently seen in adult life, especially in political and professional partnerships. . . .

"As a general principle, the smaller the group of individuals who are in competition with one another, and the narrower the range of their interests, the more intense will be the jealous attitudes developed. As the group increases in membership and their interests and activities become more varied, particular competitors normally come to occupy a less and less important place in any one individual's attention. It is as though the energy which in a restricted situation finds an outlet in one channel, perhaps, is discharged through various channels when the circle of persons and the range of interests to be reacted upon are enlarged. It is probable that most strictly social attitudes become less pronounced, though they are likely to become more habitual, according as the occasions which call them forth are multiplied.

"This principle has an interesting application to the child when he enters school. His new personal environment makes such demands upon his attention and energy, in order that he may take the first steps in adjustment thereto, that the jealous attitudes are not aroused for some time, though they are liable to appear as he begins to feel at home in the new group. The beginner is usually in the learning or adaptive attitude; he is never, at the outset, resentful towards individuals in the group who may secure greater attention than himself from the teacher or his associates. The novice in school seeks, above everything else, to win the favour of those who, for any reason, are prominent in the group. He does not normally oppose his personality to that of any one who stands well with the crowd, or who has the support of tradition in his particular expressions. . . .

"As the child grows to feel at ease in adjustment to the situations presented in the school, he commences to assume attitudes of disapproval, as well as approval, of the expressions of his associates, and even of the teacher. In due course—often by the fourth year in school, possibly earlier—he begins to manifest some feeling of jealousy towards those of his group who attain greater prominence in the work of the school than he does himself. However, according to the observations of the present writer, this feeling is not a dominant one at any period in the elementary school, except in the case of particular children who are displeased at any distinction in recitations or in conduct attained by their classmates.

"In the fourth grade of a certain elementary school of a Western city there are three backward boys who have been in this grade for two years, though they are bright enough in the things of the street. They are in a more or less hostile attitude towards all that goes on in the schoolroom, probably because they cannot succeed in it themselves, and so they would like to escape from it or destroy it. Now, they make it unpleasant, so far as they are able, for all the boys in the grade who apply themselves to their tasks and get 'good marks.' On the playground these dullards 'pick on' the 'bright' boys; and in the school they ridicule them by 'snickering' at them, or 'making faces' at them, and so on, with the result that they deter some boys from doing their best in the schoolroom. These same three ill-adjusted boys will make fun of their mates who come to school 'dressed up in fine togs.' They are themselves attired in plain clothes suited to the rough experience of the street, and they resent the adoption of different styles by any of their associates. Further, they show jealous feeling towards boys who come from 'better' homes than their own, or from more 'aristocratic' parts of the city. . . .

"It will not be necessary here to do more than to mention the chief incitement to jealousy after the beginning of the adolescent upheaval, and lasting well on into middle life. The testimony of autobiographers, as well as the observations of psychologists, indicates that rivalry for sex favours gives rise to most of the jealous attitudes of the adolescent up until full maturity is reached. Often, no doubt, it is the main cause of the jealousies of some people throughout their lives; but, normally, other and more general interests become stronger and more vital as maturity is approached. But, from the age of fifteen or sixteen on to twenty-five, or beyond, the sex needs and interests are supreme, and the individual is sensitive to sex relations above all others. No pain is so keen at this time as that which arises from slight or indifference from persons of the opposite sex, and no experience will stir an individual so deeply as that which threatens to deprive him of the exclusive possession of the affections of the one he loves."

Whatever the cause, I repeat, parents should never delay in combating repeated manifestations of jealousy, in order to make sure of preventing possible acts of extreme violence, subtle distortions of character that may persist through life, and neurotic maladies of gradual or rapid development. To bring home concretely to every parent who happens to read these lines the danger menacing his own jealous child in this last respect, I cannot do better than cite from real life a few instances of nervous trouble directly and demonstrably due to jealousy.

An eminent neurologist had for a patient a young girl whose illness took the form of frenzied, almost maniacal, outbreaks. It was necessary at times to control her forcibly, and the fear of her family was that she was on the highway to insanity, if she were not already insane. The neurologist noticed that she became most violent when her mother approached her bed. She would then cry out, strike at her mother, and wildly order her to leave the room. The mother was in despair at this behaviour, assuring the neurologist that she could not account for it, as she had always treated her daughter most affectionately—a statement which other relatives corroborated.

To get to the bottom of this mystifying case, the neurologist determined to make use of what is known as the method of dream-analysis. This method has, as a fundamental principle, the theory that most dreams, especially the dreams of childhood, represent the imaginary fulfilment of wishes which cannot be, or have not been, realised in the waking life. In the present instance, the application of dream-analysis proved most helpful. It showed that, asleep no less than when awake, the girl's mind was occupied with ideas unfavourable to her mother, and was dominated by a wish that her mother were dead. This was indicated by a number of dreams, in some of which she saw herself and her sisters dressed in mourning, while in others she was attending the funeral of women who resembled her mother.

Quite evidently a mental conflict was in progress, the girl sufficiently appreciating the sinfulness of the death—wish to resist its full emergence into consciousness, even during sleep. But its presence and persistence, as revealed by the dreams, made it clear to the physician that he was dealing, not with actual insanity, but with a case of hysteria motivated by jealousy of the mother. Further analysis disclosed an abnormal fondness for the father, in whose affections the little daughter wished to reign alone.

Sometimes the hysteria traceable to jealousy presents symptoms ingeniously calculated to compel sympathetic attention from the parent who otherwise would continue to divide his or her affections in a manner displeasing to the jealous child. Thus, a small boy became subject to attacks of severe bodily pain, which came on, usually, at night, and were relieved only when his mother took him to bed with her, sending his father to sleep in another room. In this case, and in similar cases that have been studied by medical specialists, it is not a question of conscious deceit. The pain or other hysterical symptom is wholly the result of the sentiment of jealousy having so worked on the mind of a neurotically predisposed child as to cause a subconscious fabrication of symptoms certain to gain loving care.

Likewise, some children, and particularly children of an inferior mentality or those handicapped by physical defects responsible for a seeming or real neglect of them by parents and playmates, will, under the influence of jealousy, become so disturbed nervously as to indulge in eccentricities of conduct, having for their object the compelling of the attention they feel they have been denied. For example, jealousy often is at the root of the pathological lying of neurotic children, who, on occasion, do not hesitate to bring outrageous charges against innocent persons. Their purpose is not to injure these persons; they tell their morbid lies simply because they wish to become objects of interested and sympathetic attention. For the same reason, other jealousy-dominated children sometimes concoct elaborate deceptions, notably in the way of what are called "poltergeist" performances.

From time to time newspapers report stories of haunted houses, in which small articles of furniture and bric-à-brac are flung about by mischievous ghosts—hence the name "poltergeists"—that remain invisible. When investigation is made, the "ghost" usually turns out to be a small boy or girl, who frequently is regarded as being merely a naughty child, and is punished accordingly. This is a mistake. It is not naughtiness, but hysteria. And, not infrequently, it is hysteria brought on by jealousy.[7]

President Hall, of Clark University, who has made a special study of children's lies, fittingly comments:

"Without knowing it, these hysterical girls feel disinherited and robbed of their birthright. Their bourgeoning woman's instinct to be the centre of interest and admiration bursts all bounds, and they speak and act out things which with others would be only secret reverie. Thus they can not only be appreciated but wondered at; can almost become priestesses, pythonesses, maenads, and set their mates, neighbours, or even great savants agog and agape, while they have their fling at life, reckless of consequences. Thus they can be of consequence, respected, observed, envied, perhaps even studied. So they defy their fate and wreak their little souls upon experience with abandon and have their supreme satisfaction for a day, impelled to do so by blind instinct which their intellect is too undeveloped to restrain. And all this because their actual life is so dull and empty."[8]

Nor does the mischief done by jealousy in the case of nervously inclined children stop here. It is particularly important for parents to know that there may be a postponement of its evil effects. That is, though the jealous child, while a child, may not show more than a general nervousness and may seemingly outgrow his jealousy without ill effect, it is entirely possible that in later life mental or nervous

[7] In my "Psychology and Parenthood" pp. 223-227, will be found the details of a typical poltergeist performance.

[8] "Educational Problems," vol. i, p. 363.

troubles may appear as a result of the subconscious retention of the jealous notions that have long since vanished from conscious remembrance. I might cite a number of instances strikingly illustrative of this, but will be content with giving only one—the case of a man about thirty years old, who did not dare go outdoors because he was obsessed by a fear that he would kill the first person he met in the street.

"My life," he told the physician whose aid he sought, "is one long torment. There are days when I have myself locked in my room, as I cannot venture on the street with the murderous longings that fill my mind. I spend much of my time planning alibis to escape the consequences of the murder I feel sure I shall commit. Is there any hope for me, short of imprisonment in an asylum for the dangerously insane?"

This man, as his answers to the specialist's questions made clear, was actually of a splendid character and highly cultured. His one peculiarity was this dangerous obsession. Psychological analysis to trace its origin was undertaken, and led back to his childhood. It had, as the setting giving it force and keeping it alive, a deep-seated jealousy of his father, experienced before the age of seven. More specifically, it originated in a murderous wish, entertained one day when father and son were walking together, to push his father from a mountain-top into an abyss. The child had at once recognised that this wish was wicked. He had violently repressed it, had tried to forget it, and had seemingly succeeded in doing so. But in his neurotic subconsciousness it had remained alive, to incubate and grow, until it finally blossomed into the murderous and painfully persistent obsession against people in general.

Surely, it is worth while to watch for and eradicate jealousy in childhood. Surely, too, it is worth while to develop emotional control in your children while they still are very young, and to avoid giving reason for jealousy by showing a real neglect in satisfying their natural craving for sympathy and love. On the other hand, it is equally important to avoid being over-attentive to them. This, as brought out in detail in the second chapter, is the great danger to be feared when there is only one child in the family, the exuberance of the parental love filling the child with exaggerated ideas of his own importance that are sure to be rudely jostled when he comes into contact with other children.

From these other children, as from his school teachers and casual visitors to his home, he will unconsciously demand the adulation shown by his parents. Failing to receive it, jealousy is all too apt to seize him, and, out of jealousy, nervous symptoms or character kinks are a probable result—symptoms and kinks which may, perhaps, never be entirely overcome.

What, then, is the moral of all this? What practical suggestions may be made that will help parents to cope with the problem of children's jealousy? For one thing, and most important, there must be no showing of favouritism, if you have more than one child. By your whole attitude towards your children you must make plain to them that each one ought to be, and is, equally dear to you. Of course, however, this does not mean that you should go to the foolish extreme of some parents, who carry the principle of equality so far as to give identical presents to their children. This does not serve as a corrective and preventive of jealousy; rather, it simply panders to it, and is, at bottom, a confession of helplessness on the parents' part.

The real need is to give your children a home environment of such a character that the instinct of human sympathy will be highly developed in them. Jealousy has its roots in selfishness, in an over-development of what may be called the ego-centric instinct. The jealous child is pre-eminently a child unduly occupied with thoughts of self. His personal desires and his personal interests are of paramount importance to him, just because he has not been taught that the one truly self-satisfying ideal of life is to find joy in bringing joy to others. To be sure, he cannot be taught this by direct instruction when he is very small. But indirectly, through the subtle force of suggestion, he can be taught it even then, if he is given a good parental example.

His parents themselves, not merely to prevent the budding of the sentiment of jealousy, but for the sake of the child's moral education in general, must set him an example of unselfishness. In their relations with each other, with their friends, with casual visitors to their home, they must maintain an altruistic, rather than an ego-centric, attitude. Showing true love for their child, they must—and this is especially necessary in the case of an only child—cause the child unconsciously to realise that he is not, and should not be, the sole object of their thoughts; that they have other interests, other duties in life. Unless he is constitutionally abnormal, a child brought up in such an atmosphere of general, self-forgetting kindliness is almost certain to acquire the same healthy philosophy of life that his parents have—a philosophy inimical to jealousy in every form.

As an aid to the same end, it is important to begin, at as early a time as possible, to train the child to occupy his mind actively with games and studies of educational significance. It is a fact which scarcely needs demonstration that the child in whom love of study and interest in subjects of study are developed at an early age will be a child unlikely to become unhealthily occupied with thoughts of himself. He will have too many and too strong external interests to have either time or desire for morbid self-communing.

In fine, you may set this down as certain: the more you inspire in your children external interests in play and work, doing this partly by direct teaching and partly by setting them an example of industrious activity, the less reason you will have to fear that they will fall victims to the handicap of jealousy or to the nervous maladies resultant from any form of excessive preoccupation with thoughts of self.

If, however, despite your best efforts, your child does develop jealous characteristics in marked degree, the safest and wisest thing you can do is to take him at once to a good specialist in the treatment of mental and nervous troubles. It may be that the jealousy is only the resultant of some unsuspected error of his upbringing, but it may also be symptomatic of some serious disorder requiring careful medical treatment.

CHAPTER V

SELFISHNESS

"JEALOUSY," I stated a few pages back, "has its roots in selfishness, in an over-development of what may be called the ego-centric instinct." Aside from its role as a developer of jealousy, selfishness is indeed one of the major handicaps of childhood. Moralists have long urged on parents the importance of early training to prevent their children from becoming selfish. They have rightly pictured selfishness as among the greatest of human blemishes, giving character an ugly twist and making impossible that harmonious adjustment with other people which is indispensable to individual happiness and social progress. But it is not merely to be condemned from the moralist's point of view: it also is to be condemned from the physician's. Selfishness does much more than injure character: it may even ruin the health of those afflicted with it. To put the matter briefly, training against selfishness is imperative in early life, if only as a safeguard against the functional nervous and mental maladies so common to-day.

When parents fail to teach their children to control their emotions; when they foster in them exaggerated notions of their importance by giving way to the children in everything, being over-solicitous about them, performing duties for them which the children should early be taught to perform for themselves, selfishness is an almost inevitable outgrowth. The children, in addition, may become quite unfitted to cope with the stresses of existence. And they may further become so psychically disorganised that, if after a time they no longer find themselves always having their own way, there may develop nervous symptoms which not merely are the product of an inner emotional storm, but are strangely designed to fulfil the nervous one's latent wish to remain the centre of interest and influence. Or, more bluntly stated, nervous attacks frequently are sheer manifestations of selfishness. It is selfishness that gives rise to them, and, though the victim may not be at all conscious of the fact, they represent an abnormal effort of the personality to attain selfish ends.

This is not theory. It is an established truth, and is demonstrable from the case-histories of many nervous patients, adults and children alike. And, with increasing use of the most advanced methods of mental analysis, the influence of selfishness in causing nervous ailments is certain to become more widely appreciated than it is at present. Not that selfishness is the causal factor in all nervous cases. It would be absurdly false to assert anything of the kind, but the proportion of cases in which it does figure is astonishingly high. Parents need to know this; they need to recognise that failure to curb selfishness during the formative period of childhood may mean nervous wreckage, as well as the distorting of character. In the case of a child of so-called "nervous temperament"—a child, that is to say, who begins life with an unstable nervous organisation by reason of inherited weaknesses—nervous wreckage is almost certain to be the result of neglect to take precautions against the growth of selfishness. The full effects of parental neglect in this regard may not be visible for many years, but frequently they become disconcertingly evident while the child still is young. A case reported to me by a well-known American neurologist and psychopathologist is decidedly to the point in this connection, and may well be given in some detail.

It is the case of a girl of fourteen who was brought to the neurologist because of nervous symptoms which took the form of periods of anxiety and depression, alternating with outbreaks of great irritability. The girl, her mother stated, seemed to have lost interest in everything. At times she would sit mournfully weeping; at others, fall into a passion for no apparent reason. More than once she had declared that she wanted to die. She could not, or would not, give any explanation of this most singular behaviour.

Making a diagnosis of functional, rather than organic, disease, the neurologist resorted to dream-analysis to get at the hidden causes of trouble. At his request, the girl related several dreams, all of which had the noticeable peculiarity that in them the dreamer herself was, to an unusual extent, the dominant figure of the dream-action. Another striking feature of her dreams was that many of them had to do with imaginary experiences of a painful character befalling either the dreamer's father or her brother. Mindful of the theory that dreams are directly or indirectly representative of secret wishes, the neurologist questioned his little patient about her family life. She frankly admitted that she disliked her father, and was not overfond of her brother. She disliked the father—or, as she vehemently said, "hated" him—because he scolded her. Her coldness towards her brother arose from the fact that her mother had fallen into the habit of tactlessly holding him up as a model of good behaviour.

"I love my mother, though," she added, "because she is good to me, and generally lets me do what I want."

Summoning the mother to a private conference, the physician learned that, from early childhood, his patient had been very obstinate and self-willed. Her mother, through mistaken affection, had pampered her. She had literally made herself a slave to the daughter, even to the extent of giving up evening engagements that she might sit by her daughter's bed, gently stroking her head until she fell asleep.

"She cannot sleep unless I do this," said the mother, "and though I have lately tried to discontinue it, I cannot, because she cries and shrieks until I come to her."

To the neurologist the situation was now perfectly clear. The daughter's nervous symptoms were manifestly the not surprising reaction of a personality untrained in emotional control and unexpectedly confronted by a novel and painful state of affairs—the mother's half-hearted attempt to break away from her self-imposed slavery. However, it would hardly do to tell the mother that her early mismanagement of the child was responsible for the neurotic condition which had developed, and that this neurotic condition was, in reality, only a subconsciously originated device to reassert the daughter's waning authority over her mother. What the neurologist did say was:

"Madam, if you want your daughter to get well, you must at once stop this practice of stroking her to sleep. I must ask you to begin to-night. Send your daughter to her room, leave her in bed, shut and lock the door, and let her shriek. This may seem hard and cruel, but it is actually a greater kindness than a continuance of the stroking would be. It is, indeed, a first and necessary step in her cure."

The mother obeyed. For two nights the house resounded with the girl's cries. The third night she went to bed and to sleep without a protest. Then the physician once more sent for the mother.

"You are soon leaving town for the summer, I understand," he said. "What are you going to do with your daughter?"

"Why, take her with us, of course."

"You must do nothing of the sort. Instead, send her to a girls' camp. She needs contact with other girls; she needs the discipline such contact will give her. It is far and away the best medicine she can have. Her recovery depends solely on her developing a new point of view, a mental outlook that will extend beyond herself. This is what a good camp for girls can give her."

The outcome vindicated his words. That fall the nervously depressed girl came back from a summer in camp radiantly happy and with a vastly altered disposition. Since then her parents have had no trouble with her.

Please, however, understand clearly that she was really a sick girl when her mother took her to my neurological friend. It was not simply a question of dealing with a "naughty" girl. The depression, the tears, the attacks of irritability were not deliberately put on to excite sympathy and to play on the mother's affections. This assuredly was their basic purpose, but they were the product of subconscious, not conscious, mental action. They were the resultant of an emotional stress, the responsibility for which rested not with the girl herself but with her mother's unwise treatment of her. If she had become neurotic, it was because her mother had made her so. What she needed, and all she needed, was psychic re-education, and this she obtained through the neurologist's common-sense method of cure.

The fact that such cases are indicative, not of mere naughtiness, but of the action of an inner force operating independently of the victim's conscious volition, will become more apparent when I add that sometimes the symptoms causing medical aid to be invoked are physical instead of mental. In one typical case of this sort a neurologist was summoned to examine a small boy who had been attacked by a peculiar weakness of the legs. To all appearance, he was in perfect bodily health, but when he attempted to walk his legs gave way, and he would fall, unless quickly supported. The most careful testing failed to reveal any organic cause for this condition, and a diagnosis of juvenile hysteria was made. It was learned that the boy's trouble began soon after he had met in the street a badly crippled, semi-paralysed man, whose appearance had evidently made a deep impression on his mind, as he spoke of it, when he got home, in terms partly of astonishment and partly of fear. There could be no doubt that the sight of this man had acted as a "suggestion" to cause the development of a somewhat similar condition in the boy himself. The question remained, why should the mere seeing of a crippled man have sufficient suggestive force to bring on an hysterical crippling? For undoubtedly the boy must have had not a few equally distressing experiences long before this one.

On investigation it turned out that at the time he saw the cripple he was under considerable mental strain. A petted, spoiled child, he had rebelled against being sent to school. He would much rather stay home and play by himself or with his mother. His parents' desires in the matter were as nothing to him: it was what he wanted that was the important thing. For once, though, the parents insisted on being obeyed by their thoroughly selfish boy. He had to go to school, and go to school he did, until the hysterical paralysis set in. This paralysis, of course, was somewhat inconvenient, since it limited his opportunities for play, but it at least had the advantage of keeping him from attending the school that he detested. The boy himself was not in the slightest conscious of the part thus played by selfish wishing in the development of his diseased condition. He was really frightened at finding himself unable to stand and walk. Nevertheless, so strong was his antipathy against school that it was some time before the suggestion of paralysis was broken down by appropriate psychotherapeutic treatment.

Other cases even more extraordinary are recorded in medical annals. One "spoiled child," a little girl not five years old, had a series of convulsive attacks, following the unexpected refusal of her parents to grant a request that involved risk to her if they granted it. After the convulsions she was paralysed in her lower limbs, and the parents, terrified, called in an eminent specialist in nervous diseases. Fortunately, the specialist recognised almost at once that it was a case of hysterical paralysis, brought on by lack of discipline and lack of training in emotional control, and he obtained the parents' permission to isolate the little girl and treat her as he deemed best. His treatment was harsh, but exceedingly effective. For two days he starved the child, then put a bowl of bread and milk some distance from her bed. The suggestion of food was too strong for the suggestion of paralysis. Without further ado, she skipped nimbly out of bed and secured the bowl. But the specialist did not reproach her for being a naughty girl. His reproaches were for the parents, to whom he gave some greatly needed advice as to her future upbringing.

Hysterical pains, contractures, swellings, even hysterical blindness, have been observed in children who, after having been unduly indulged, feel that their father or mother, as the case may be, is no longer as attentive to and lenient with them as they would like. More frequently, under such conditions, the symptoms of nervousness are chiefly mental, or, if physical, are confined to muscular twitchings, slight involuntary movements of the face, head, hands, and similar manifestations. Unhappily, the true significance of these is often overlooked. They are thought to be defects which the child will "outgrow," and in many cases they certainly are outgrown, to all appearance. But, if the moral weaknesses underlying them—the self-centredness, the deficiency in emotional control—are not in the meantime corrected, at any crisis in adult life there is likely to result a nervous breakdown or a serious attack of hysteria. Indeed, in not a few cases of adult hysteria, the causal agency of selfishness is unmistakably in evidence to those accustomed to interpreting nervous symptoms. There are plenty of men and women whose chronic neuroticism is motivated by a subconscious craving to be the centre of attraction, or to be perpetually dominant in the family life. There are other unfortunates who, when their will is seriously crossed, take refuge, like the boys and girls just mentioned, in various forms of nervous disease. The curious experience of a New England physician, Doctor A. Myerson, for some time connected with the Boston Psychopathic Hospital, is by no means as unique as might be thought.

This physician was summoned to attend a woman suffering from what was supposed to be a cerebral hemorrhage. She no longer was able to move her right arm, right leg, or the right side of her face, and had entirely lost the power of speech. For many months previous to the onset of this deplorable condition she had been troubled at irregular intervals by headaches, nausea, and fainting spells. The patient herself and her friends had little doubt that she was in so serious a condition that recovery could not be expected. But Doctor Myerson, making use of the most up-to-date methods of neurological diagnosis, soon was able to reach a reassuring verdict. It was a case, he found, not of organic, but of functional paralysis—in fine, a case of hysteria. And, in the end, by employing what is technically known as the method of "indirect suggestion," he actually re-educated the paralyzed woman both to walk and to talk.

Meantime, he made a searching inquiry to ascertain just why she had been stricken by hysterical paralysis. He discovered, for one thing, that the patient's fainting and vomiting spells and her headaches had usually followed bitter quarrels with her husband—and usually had the effect of placing victory on her side. There was one point, nevertheless, on which the husband was immovable. He was a poor man and could not grant his wife's insistent demand to move to a more expensive neighbourhood. He would not have granted it if he could, for in the particular neighbourhood to which she wished to move she had friends whom he regarded as undesirable. It appeared that the attack of paralysis and speechlessness had been preceded by an exceptionally bitter quarrel over this question of moving—"a quarrel which," to quote from Doctor Myerson's report, "had lasted for a whole day and into the night of the attack."

Thus, the attack itself could be correctly interpreted as the supreme effort of a self-centred, neurotic personality to gain a desired end. But, while making this interpretation, Doctor Myerson was quick to add, in his report on the case, that the attack had not by any means been brought on through the patient's "conscious purpose or volition." It was all an affair of her subconsciousness, working in a blind, abnormal, irrational way to help attain the object of her conscious desire. That her subconsciousness should work so abnormally and so disastrously was chiefly due, beyond any doubt, to the absence of adequate training in self-control and emotional restraint.

But it is not only as a strange, irrational mode of fulfilling a wish that hysteria and other nervous disorders may become manifest in selfish people. Without this element of wishing entering in at all, nervousness is particularly likely to attack the selfish. Many nervous conditions are directly brought on by conscious or subconscious fixing of the thoughts on the bodily processes. We are so constituted that our internal organs work best when we pay no attention to them—or, more strictly, when we pay no attention to the physical sensations to which they give rise while working. If, for any reason, our attention is turned to and held on these sensations, they at once become exaggerated, and the organs giving rise to them tend to function badly. In this way any bodily organ may be disturbed in its action, and general symptoms of nervousness result through nothing but over-attention.

An eminent New York physician, Doctor J. J. Walsh, who has given special thought to this aspect of the problem of nervousness, states the case more fully, as follows:

"If something has particularly attracted a patient's attention to some part of his anatomy, and if his attention is concentrated on it and allowed to dwell long on it, his feelings may be so exaggerated as to tempt him to think that they are connected with some definite pathological condition, and he may even translate them into serious portents of organic disease. If a patient once begins to waste nervous energy on himself because of solicitude with regard to these symptoms, then it will not be long before feelings of tiredness, incapacity for work, at times insomnia and certain disturbances of memory, are likely to be noted. Then the neurasthenic picture seems to be complete.

"This is the process so picturesquely called 'short-circuiting,' by which nervous energy exhausts itself upon the individual himself instead of in the accomplishment of external work. Many of the worst cases of so-called neurasthenia have their origin in this process. It is true that this set of events is much more likely to occur among people of lowered nervous vitality, but, under certain conditions, it may develop in those who are otherwise in good health up to the moment when the attention happened to be particularly called to certain feelings. The physician can start these patients off anew, after improving their physical condition, if he can only bring them to see how much their concentration of mind upon themselves is the cause of their symptoms."[9]

Now, of all people likely to be thus afflicted, the selfish man or woman is by all means the likeliest, simply because his or her every mode of thinking revolves about self. It is the selfish man's wishes, his pleasures, his grievances, his reverses, that are of supreme importance to him. When, moreover, his early upbringing has been such as to leave him sadly short in emotional control, any passing disturbance in the workings of his internal organs may easily hold disastrous consequences for him. He worries over little ailments—as, for example, a slight attack of indigestion—to which people of less self-centred nature would give little or no thought. And, by his persistent worrying and his persistent over-attention to the way his stomach works, it may not be long before he has become a victim of chronic nervous dyspepsia.

[9] "Psychotherapy," pp. 559-560.

Of course, unselfish people who are lacking in emotional control, or carry about with them the unassimilated memory of childhood emotional shocks, may likewise become nervous invalids of one sort or another. But they are much less likely to do this than selfish people are, if only because the unselfish are not so eternally occupied with themselves. They have externalised their thoughts; they have neither time nor inclination to think about trivial aches and pains. Unless overwhelmed by an unexpected emotional shock—for instance, by the sudden death of a beloved relative or by the shock of some great fright—they are likely to go through life comfortably and normally enough. On the other hand, the selfish person is always in danger of becoming morbidly introspective, with resultant damage to the functioning of his nervous system.

Besides all this, there is the important consideration that to be selfish means to be unhappy. Even if actual nervous ailments of a serious sort are escaped by the selfish, unhappiness in the social relations and in the *family* relations is certain to be experienced. It is my firm belief that, more than any other single cause, selfishness is responsible for misunderstandings and increasing bitterness between husband and wife, ending all too often in a breakdown of the sacred institution of marriage. To deal successfully with that dread problem of to-day—the divorce evil—we must, I submit, first appreciate how basic in marriage failure is the factor of selfishness. To this theme I now invite the attention of my parent-readers, for it is a theme of particular interest to them. If I am correct, it is through education for marriage and, most of all, through education against selfishness that the divorce problem can most surely he solved.

What a problem it is! And a problem that has been steadily growing in seriousness. In the twenty years from 1867 to 1886, according to figures compiled by the United States Census Bureau, 328,716 divorces were granted throughout the country. In the next twenty years—that is, from 1887 to 1906—divorces aggregated the enormous total of 945,625. In other words, in a period of only twenty years nearly two million men and women in the United States had their marriage ties legally severed, the break-up being at the rate of about one hundred and thirty divorces a day.

And this increase has been progressively growing year after year. In 1867 there were only 9,937 divorces for the entire country. In 1906 no fewer than 72,012 divorces were granted. Four years ago an unofficial estimate put the annual divorce crop at nearly one hundred thousand, or, roughly, one hundred divorces for every one hundred thousand of population. The same estimate indicated that one marriage in every twelve ends in divorce.

Nor do these figures afford a complete view of the extent to which marital infelicity obtains in the United States. Every year thousands of marriages virtually, or actually, terminate without recourse to the courts. Men and women who have entered into the marriage state really in love with each other, develop so-called "incompatibilities of temperament" which transform love into indifference, even hate. Reluctant to seek divorce—perhaps conscientiously opposed to it—they continue to live together, husband and wife in name only, or they arrange a voluntary separation. Many others escape from what they have come to regard as an intolerable yoke by the easy expedient of desertion, not necessarily followed by court proceedings. It is impossible to give exact figures, but unquestionably the number of marriages which collapse in divorce is a comparatively small proportion of all unhappy marriages.

Taking the increase in divorce, however, as a concrete, definite measure of marriage failure, the problem of explanation and remedy remains obviously and sufficiently urgent. And it must be said that as a rule the offered solutions are either evasive or superficial.

Some investigators, despairing of finding any solution, insist that the increase in divorce is an unavoidable product of the complex, strenuous life of modern civilisation. Others, much of the same mind, advocate "trial marriages" as a palliative. Still others, singularly lacking in courtesy, or of a myopic vision so far as women are concerned, throw the blame on the "feminist movement," on the increasing emancipation of woman from her old-time position of slavish inferiority. Finally, there are investigators who, noting that the increase in divorce has steadily been gaining momentum since the Civil War, attribute this to the difference in economic conditions before and after the war. In effect, they say that there are more divorces because the country is wealthier, the inference being that increased national prosperity has had an unsettling effect on the national life.

That this contention is sound cannot be gainsaid; but it does not go deep enough. Of itself, it no more explains the increase in divorce than it does the increase in crime and the increase in mental and nervous disease, equally in evidence since the Civil War. These, too, there is warrant for affirming, have increased because of changed economic conditions. It remains, however, to ascertain the precise factor or factors brought into operation by this economic change to account for the growth in crime, insanity, nervous troubles, and divorce. And, in this connection, it is most interesting and important to observe that, so far as concerns crime, insanity, and nervous troubles, recent research has made clear exactly why there has been an increase and how this may best be checked.

It is now recognised that, psychologically speaking, crime, insanity, and nervousness represent an imperfect adaptation to the environment in which the criminal, the lunatic, or the nervous person lives. This failure of adaptation may be due either to inborn lack of capacity to meet the requirements of the environment, or to lack of proper training.

Not so many years ago it was the consensus of scientific opinion that in most cases of crime, insanity and nervousness the victim was hopelessly handicapped from the start by the nature of his being. There was much talk of "inherited criminality," "congenital brain defects," and "neuropathic inheritance." But observation and experiment have compelled an almost complete abandonment of this doctrine of fatal degeneration. To-day scientists largely hold that not more than 1 or 2 per cent. of criminals can be stigmatised as criminals by birth; that insanity is not inheritable, like eye-colour or hair-colour; and that nervousness is, at bottom, an acquired, rather than inherited, disorder.

Accordingly, if crime, insanity, and nervousness are on the increase, it follows that faults of training, rather than innate and unescapable tendencies, are the responsible factors. More specifically, crime, insanity, and nervousness have increased because no adequate effort has been made, by appropriate training, to fit the individual to withstand the extra strain put upon him by the economic changes of the past half century.

Still further, modern scientific research has discovered the specific training fault which, more than anything else, accounts for the failure in adaptation. Stated briefly, this fault consists in neglect to develop moral and emotional control during the first years of life.

In the case of criminality it has been proved, by repeated experiment tried on a large scale,[10] that even the descendants of a long line of criminals, if carefully trained in early childhood, will lead upright lives. In the case of insanity, the discovery that the three principal causes of mental disease are excessive indulgence in alcohol, sexual indiscretions, and emotional stress, points directly to the importance of training, aimed at the development of moral control. But most impressive, as emphasising the need for beginning this training at an early age, is the evidence accumulated in the case of those functional maladies, hysteria, neurasthenia, and psychasthenia—evidence which we have already discussed in much detail in these pages.

Study the history of every case of "nervous breakdown," of psychasthenic fear, of hysterical anxiety and disabilities, of neurasthenic aches and pains, and there will always be found a background of emotional intensity and self-centredness, persisting from early childhood. Hence, the demand of the modern neurologist and medical psychologist for training in youth that will foster control of the emotions and that will habituate the individual to forget self in useful activities. "The mind occupied with external interests will have neither time nor inclination to feed upon itself."

If, therefore, the one sure check to the increase in crime, insanity, and nervous disorders is moral training in early life, can it be doubted that the same process offers the strongest means of checking the tendency to flood the divorce courts?

Ninety-nine divorces out of every hundred, it is safe to say, result from errors of thinking and living—errors directly traceable to shortcomings in early training. Selfishness and lack of control—these, I insist, are the usual elements out of which divorces grow. And what are these but bad habits, for which good habits might have been substituted had proper precautions been taken by the parents in the plastic, formative period of youth? Even in respect to the sexual phase of marriage—that phase in which so many marriages come to grief—the trouble, when trouble occurs, may, in most cases, be wholly attributed to parental thoughtlessness or ignorance. On the sexual side, as on all sides of married life, the great need is for education for marriage.

It is not my intention here to go into details. It must suffice to say that investigation has shown that the sexual impulse begins to manifest itself in sundry ways far earlier than most parents appreciate, and that unless care is taken to observe

[10] See "Psychology and Parenthood," pp. 8-18.

and offset eccentricities of behaviour possibly containing a sexual element, permanent harm may result.

For example, there often is a sexual element in the cruelty with which not a few children treat play-fellows or household pets. The exaggerated affection little boys sometimes display for their mothers, and little girls for their fathers, is to-day likewise regarded by many medical psychologists as a sexual signal calling for educational measures to insure a more even distribution of affection for both parents. These same psychologists insist that at the first obvious signs of interest in sexual matters—as when the child begins to ask questions about his origin—he should be given frank, if tactful, elementary instruction in the facts of sex. Recall the quotation previously made from Havelock Ellis in this connection. Evasive or untruthful answers will not do. They only fix the attention more strongly on the subject, and from this fixing of the attention a dangerously morbid interest in things sexual may develop.

Clearly, parents who would do their full duty by their children have no easy task before them. Yet everything combines to show that unless they make a business of parenthood—and, in especial, unless, by direct instruction and the force of good example, they develop in their children the virtues of self-control and self-forgetfulness—the after lives of those children, when themselves married, will be anything but happy, and may, in addition, be lives marred by some form of serious nervous or mental disturbance.

CHAPTER VI

BASHFULNESS AND INDECISION

DOCTOR W. BECHTEREW, a distinguished Russian physician, was one day visited by a man of extraordinary appearance. Cheap and shabby clothing fitted the visitor's gaunt frame badly; his gait was shuffling; his whole form and manner testified pathetically to an overwhelming burden of poverty, anxiety, and dread. But what was most remarkable about him was a pair of enormous black spectacles, giving a horribly grotesque aspect to his pallid, bearded face. It was with difficulty that Doctor Bechterew concealed the astonishment he felt and courteously inquired what he could do for his strange visitor.

"I have come," was the hesitating, almost stammering, reply, "in the hope that you can cure me of my bashfulness."

"Your bashfulness?" repeated the physician, with a quizzical, but kindly, smile. "Is that all that troubles you?"

"It is enough," answered the other, vehemently. "Doctor, it has made life a hell for me."

"And for how long have you been bashful?"

"Virtually since childhood. I can positively place its beginnings in my schooldays." His words now flowed swiftly, torrentially. "Long before I left school I noticed that I felt awkward and uneasy when anybody looked directly at me. I found myself blushing, stammering, turning away, unable to look people in the eye.

"After I left school and went to work, matters became much worse. In business I had to meet strangers all the time, and in the presence of strangers I felt absolutely helpless. My bashfulness increased to such an extent that I began to invent excuses to stay away from my work, and to remain at home in a miserable solitude. But this did not do; I had to earn my living. In desperation, I hit on the idea of wearing these black spectacles."

"So that people cannot see your eyes?"

"Exactly. They have helped me wonderfully; intrenched behind them, I feel comparatively safe. But I detest them, and I long to be like other men. Is there no cure for me?"

Bizarre, startlingly unique as this must seem, it, after all, differs only in the single detail of the spectacles from hundreds of other cases which might be cited. All over the world are men and women who suffer agonies from an oppressive, and to them inexplicable, sense of timidity when brought into contact with other people. Many, to be sure, make a brave effort to conceal the true state of affairs, compelling themselves to mingle more or less freely in society, despite the torturing apprehensions they then feel. Others of less stubborn mould either seclude themselves or deliberately choose careers that leave them much in solitude. Sometimes, for that matter, the choosing of such careers is an affair not of choice, but of necessity. A man of thirty-four confided to his physician, Doctor Paul Hartenberg:

"I began life as an assistant to my father in the wholesale liquor business, my work being such that I did not realise my extreme bashfulness. But it was made very clear to me when, owing to my father's failure, I was obliged to seek employment elsewhere.

"I applied for and was given the position of manager in a large café. It was part of my duty to keep order among the employees, and, to my dismay, I found that I was not equal to this. Whenever I had to exert my authority I was strangely embarrassed; I stammered, trembled, and, worst of all, blushed like a girl. The employees, as you may imagine, were not long in perceiving how timid and bashful I was, and affairs rapidly came to such a pass that the owner of the café angrily dismissed me.

"I then became a clerk in a department store. But, alas! my deplorable bashfulness was again my undoing. If a customer looked at me when asking a question or giving an order, I blushed, became so embarrassed that I had to turn away, and, in my confusion, paid no attention to what the customer was saying. If the latter repeated his words I became more disturbed than ever, trembled, perspired, and acted so queerly that people thought I was drunk.

"Again I was dismissed, and again I found employment, this time in a smaller store. The result was the same. Thus I passed from position to position, always descending in the social scale. What do you suppose I am doing at present? I am washing dishes in the cellar of a restaurant. It is not pleasant work, but it at least shelters me from the terrible gaze of strangers."

This, fortunately, is an exceptional case. Yet it is certain that many a man is to-day holding a position far below that for which he really has ability, simply because he is too bashful to assert himself, dreading not so much the increased responsibilities of more remunerative work as the fact that it will bring him more conspicuously and intimately into the view of other people. He feels in his soul, poor fellow, that the result will be to plunge him into unendurable confusion. It is an ordeal too great for him to face, and he clings desperately to the inferior position, which, from his distorted point of view, has the merit of allowing him to go through life unnoticed and, consequently, untroubled.

What, then, is this bashfulness which exerts so widespread and baneful an influence? Whence does it take its rise? And how is its victim to go about the task of overcoming it? These are questions of vital significance, particularly in this age of complex civilisation and strenuous competition, in which the bashful man is at a tremendous disadvantage. Happily, he appreciates this, and resorts with increasing frequency to the physician's office in quest of advice and aid. As a result, far more is known about bashfulness to-day than was ever the case before, albeit in its most important aspects as yet known only to a comparatively small number of psychologically trained physicians.

These physicians recognise that there are two distinct types of bashfulness, the one chronic, the other occasional, both of which represent an abnormal exaggeration of the shyness which is a normal characteristic of nearly every child, and which manifests itself in blushing, fidgeting, hiding the face, etc. Ordinarily, this organic shyness, as the psychologist Baldwin has termed it, disappears between the fifth and seventh year. But it may recur under special conditions, and it is specially likely to recur, as almost everybody knows from experience, under conditions focusing public attention on the person. Under such conditions—being called on unexpectedly to speak in public, taking part for the first time in theatrical performances, and so forth—bashfulness of the occasional type is very much in evidence, its symptoms ranging from tremor, palpitation, and vasomotor disturbances to the paralysis of "stage fright." Neither psychologically nor medically is this type of bashfulness of much importance. As the novelty of the conditions giving rise to it wears off—when, for example, one has become accustomed to public speaking—it usually disappears. Like the organic shyness of childhood, it is merely a product of inexperience, an expression of an instinctive reaction that is possibly "a far-off echo from the dim past, when fear of the unknown was a safeguard in the struggle for existence."

Altogether different is the case with those who are habitually bashful, of whom the world holds many thousands. Here, obviously, some factor or factors other than inexperience must enter to cause the chronic timidity which has the special quality of afflicting its victim only when in the presence of other human beings. This, indeed, is the distinguishing characteristic of bashfulness, as was pointed out long ago by Charles Darwin, in his statement that bashfulness seems to depend on "sensitiveness to the opinion, whether good or bad, of others." Darwin also held—and his view still is the prevailing one—that the sensitiveness of the habitually bashful man relates mostly to external appearances. That is to say, he is bashful because he knows he is awkward, because he is dressed out of style or not in keeping with the special occasion, or because he suffers from some real or fancied bodily defect. To the objection that there are plenty of awkward, badly dressed, and physically deformed men and women who are not at all bashful, the advocates of this theory fall back on heredity as the ultimate determining factor, insisting that it is an inborn weakness which makes the bashful man or woman supersensitive to the opinion of others regarding his or her personal appearance and demeanour.

Now, recent research seems to leave no doubt that heredity does operate to some extent in the causation of bashfulness, since most bashful persons—at any rate, among those who come under the care of physicians—have a strain of the neurotic in their family histories. On the other hand, it has been quite as positively established that the matter of external appearances has a causal relation to bashfulness in comparatively few cases, though it may act as an aggravating element. In case after case the first manifestations of true chronic bashfulness have been traced to a period in life far antedating any anxiety on the person's part respecting the way he walks or dresses or looks. More than this, when the bashful themselves are questioned as to the causes of their bashfulness, they usually either profess entire ignorance, or emphasise mental, rather than physical, factors.

"I attribute my bashfulness to no physical cause," is a characteristic response. "I attribute it to a certain weakness of mind, to my lack of self-confidence, to fear of ridicule, and especially to a nervous excitement which I feel whenever others look at me."

Of course, apart from the doubt which such a response casts on the external appearances theory of bashfulness, and its emphasis on the mental, as opposed to the physical, factor, it really throws scarcely any light on the question of causation. Just as there are many awkward, badly dressed, and deformed people who are not bashful, so there are many modest and sensitive ones who go through life in wholly normal fashion, perhaps untroubled even by bashfulness of the occasional type. Quite evidently there still is an underlying something which has to be taken into account before one can fully understand chronic bashfulness.

That something the modern medical psychologist is beginning to believe he has discovered through proceeding on the assumption that bashfulness is far more than a mere innate weakness or character defect; that it is, in reality, a functional nervous trouble, differing only in degree, not in kind, from hysteria and other psychoneuroses. That is to say, the medical psychologist assumes that, as is now believed to be the case in every psychoneurosis, the bashful man is the victim of subconscious memories of distressing incidents in his early life; incidents which, in his case, have had the effect of arousing in an exaggerated degree sentiments of shame or fear.

The supersensitive child, having seen or heard something that profoundly shocks him, or having committed some petty or really serious fault, feels, on the one hand, that he has a shameful secret he must guard carefully, and, on the other hand, fears that people can read his secret in his eyes. Hence, he develops feelings of awkwardness and embarrassment when others look at and speak to him. He fidgets, blushes, stammers, trembles; in a word, displays all the symptoms indicated by the term bashfulness. In the course of time one of two things will happen: either increased knowledge will reassure him, and he will, as the saying is, outgrow his bashfulness; or the hidden fear and shame—even though the original occasion for them may have completely lapsed from conscious remembrance—will fix themselves firmly in his mind, causing a habit of bashfulness which may torture him all his life.

Whether this new theory as to bashfulness of the chronic type holds good invariably, it is as yet impossible to say. Certainly, it has been verified in an astonishingly large number of cases. Time and again, applying some one of the delicate methods by which they tunnel into the most obscure recesses of the mind, medical psychologists have dragged into the full light of conscious recollection forgotten memories which the victims of bashfulness themselves recognise as connected with the onset of their abnormal timidity. Often their bashfulness completely disappears, or is markedly abated, as soon as the memories responsible for it are recovered. Or, when an immediate cure is not wrought, one is pretty sure to result after an explanation of the evolution of the trouble and the application of appropriate suggestions to develop self-confidence and will power.

To illustrate by citing a few instances from life, let me give first the case of a young New England man, who, as usually happens, did not resort to a physician until his bashfulness had begun to interfere with his earning a livelihood.

"I have not the slightest idea what is the matter with me," he told the neurologist whom he consulted, "but the fact is that for a good many years I have felt strangely timid when meeting people. I believe I am naturally of a courageous disposition—certainly I do not suffer from cowardice in the ordinary sense—but I actually blush and tremble if spoken to suddenly or looked at intently. Lately I notice this has been growing worse."

"Can you tell me," the physician asked, "just when you first noticed that you were bashful?"

"No, I am sorry to say I can't. I only know that it began while I was a boy."

Nevertheless, by the aid of a method of psychoanalysis, or psychological mind-tunnelling, it was ascertained that, subconsciously, he did know exactly when his bashfulness began, and also was well aware of its cause. From among the forgotten, or only vaguely remembered, episodes of his boyhood there emerged, with exceptional vividness, a memory-picture of the time when he first went to work. He recalled with painful intensity the figure of his employer, a stern, cold, hard man, with piercing eyes.

"Those eyes seemed to be on me everywhere I went. They seemed to be watching for the least mistake I might make. I began to wonder what would happen to me if I did make mistakes. Then I began to feel incompetent and to fear that he would notice my incompetency. I grew nervous, awkward, timid. Whenever he spoke to me, I jumped, I blushed, I trembled. After a time I did the same when anybody spoke to me."

"And sometimes you still think of that first employer who frightened you so much?"

"I try not to, but I know I do."

To the neurologist the cause of his patient's bashfulness was now evident. The fear, the anxiety, the over-conscientiousness engendered by the employer's attitude, working in the mind of an ultra-impressionable boy, were quite enough to initiate a habit of abnormal diffidence. Tactfully, the physician made this clear to the patient; earnestly he impressed on him the idea that the unpleasant experience of which he spoke was a thing of the past, and was nothing of which he now need stand in dread; and tirelessly he reiterated the suggestion that the patient had it in his own power to exorcise the demon of bashfulness created by the painful subconscious memory-image of those early days. In the end he had the satisfaction of sending him on his way rejoicing in a perfect cure.

Strikingly different in its inception is a case that came under the observation of Doctor Bechterew. In this instance the patient was a young woman of excellent family and most attractive appearance. The symptom of which she chiefly complained was an abnormal blushing. When with the members of her own family, no less than with strangers, she would, at the least provocation, feel the blood suffusing her face and would turn distressingly red. To avoid this, she kept much to herself, and led a lonely, miserable life.

Questioned by Doctor Bechterew as to the length of time she had been thus afflicted, and any prior occurrences which might have given her a real and urgent reason for embarrassment and blushing, her answers at first were wholly unenlightening. But little by little, probing with the skill of the trained psychological cross-examiner, he drew from her the details of a pathetic experience.

At the age of seventeen, it appeared, she had been thrown much into the company of a married man old enough to be her father. A friendship had sprung up between them, but, on her part, there had certainly been no thought of anything beyond friendship, until one evening at a garden party he asked her to walk with him in a secluded part of the grounds.

"While we were talking together," she confided to Doctor Bechterew, "he suddenly asked me if I cared for him—if I cared enough to leave home and spend the rest of my life with him. His avowal of love shocked and shamed me. I hastily left him and, with burning cheeks, rejoined the other guests.

"As soon as possible, I made my excuses and went home. It seemed to me that my face betrayed my secret. Afterwards I could not speak to or even think of that man without blushing. Now that you have made me recall the circumstance, I feel sure that out of that terrible experience has gradually been developed the habit of bashfulness and blushing which has made life almost unbearable to me."

Contrast with this a third case: the case of a young Jew, robust and alert-looking, a wagon driver by occupation, who applied to the Vanderbilt Clinic in New York City to be treated for what he vaguely termed a "nervous trouble." Referred to Doctor A. A. Brill, already mentioned as a specialist in nervous disorders, he confessed that the malady for which he sought relief was nothing more or less than bashfulness.

"It may seem strange to you," said he, "that a fellow like me should be bashful, but I am so timid when with strangers that I scarcely know what I am doing. I speak and act like a fool; my hands tremble; I trip over things."

"Can you give any reason why you should feel so awkward and embarrassed?"

"Not the slightest. I often have tried to explain it to myself, but all to no purpose. As far as I can tell, it is without a cause."

"Still, it must have a cause, and we will do our best to discover what that is."

Step by step, in the course of several days' investigation by psychoanalysis, Doctor Brill led the patient through the details of his past life. In this way it was definitely ascertained that the bashfulness of which he complained dated from his twelfth year. Delving among the forgotten memories of that early period, Doctor Brill presently unearthed one which the patient, the moment he recalled it, recognised as being coincidental with the beginning of the excessive timidity that had brought him such suffering.

It was the memory of a boyhood escapade that had at the time caused unusual remorse, shame, and fear of discovery. He had fancied that others could read in his eyes what he had done; he became afraid to look at people or to have them look at him. Awkwardness, embarrassment, bashfulness grew apace, and remained characteristic of him even after he had forgotten all about the affair from which they sprang.

Thanks, however, to the recovery of this lost memory-image, and of other subconscious reminiscences which had intensified the feeling of shame, it was now possible for Doctor Brill to institute psychotherapeutic treatment that eventually resulted in a cure. Incidentally, it also resulted in materially improving the young man's position in life. Freed from his bashfulness, he developed unexpected ambition, and eventually became the owner of a well-paying business.

Similarly, boyhood weaknesses and failings, carrying with them profound feelings of shame and apprehension, were found responsible for the bashfulness experienced by Doctor Hartenberg's dish-washing patient and Doctor Bechterew's visitor with the black spectacles.

Always, in truth, the story seems to be the same: there has been in the chronically bashful man's early life some specific shock, fright, or anxiety, which, provoking in a supersensitive mind feelings of extreme embarrassment, has established a bashfulness that may not fully yield to any method of treatment until the remote and usually forgotten cause is recalled to remembrance.

Happily, this requirement is not always necessary. As an eminent medical psychologist once said to me:

"It is my experience that, in many cases, a cure can be brought about simply by developing the patient's will power, either through suggestion in hypnosis, or through psychic re-education in the normal waking state. In such instances, it is enough to explain to the patient that his bashfulness undoubtedly had its origin in some shock which he has forgotten; that while, in the beginning, he may have had reason enough for feeling bashful, that reason has long since been outlived; and that his present bashfulness is actually nothing more than a bad habit, the result of self-suggestion.

"Attacking the problem this way and applying strong counter-suggestion, it frequently is possible to effect a cure without a tedious preliminary ransacking of subconscious memories. When, however, this method fails, psychoanalytic investigation becomes indispensable."

Manifestly of even greater importance than the cure of bashfulness is its prevention. This, on any theory of its causation, and especially on the view here advanced, is primarily a matter resting with parents. The appearance in a growing boy or girl of symptoms of habitual uneasiness and embarrassment when with other children or older persons should be regarded as a reason for real anxiety. Actually, however, as in the case of children who show extreme or persistent jealousy, most parents are inclined to dismiss such symptoms from their minds with the careless remark, "Yes, he's bashful; but that's nothing. He'll outgrow it." Unfortunately, he may not outgrow it without definite aid and guidance.

For one thing, the effort should immediately be made to develop in him interests, whether scholastic or athletic—preferably both—that will take him out of himself. Whatever else may be said of bashfulness, it is always, like selfishness, a sign of excessive preoccupation, conscious or unconscious, with thoughts of self. The bashful boy, no less than the bashful man, is abnormally self-centred. And, besides endeavouring to weaken his extreme egoism, there should be a systematic attempt to cultivate self-control and self-reliance; while, at the same time, his confidence should be tactfully sought, to draw from him a statement as to anything that is particularly perplexing or worrying him, and thereby to gain a vantage point for effectually banishing doubt and anxiety from his mind.

To banish doubt and anxiety from his mind! I am put in remembrance of another serious life handicap, allied to bashfulness in having as a basic element lack of self-reliance and self-confidence, and, like bashfulness, originating in childhood experiences. This handicap is the habit of futile doubting and reasoning, whether about matters of importance or matters of no importance. In some people the habit of futile doubting is so extreme as to amount to a veritable disease. Again, let me make use of an instance from real life to bring out concretely the condition I have in mind.

To a neurologist in the city of Washington there came a man thirty years of age. There was nothing in his appearance to set him apart from other people. He was intelligent-looking, well dressed, well mannered, and he did not seem at all out of health. But this, in effect, is what he said to the neurologist:

"Doctor, I have come to you as a last resort, and if you cannot help me I do not know what I shall do. I am mentally all in pieces. My mind is so weak that I cannot even decide what clothes I ought to put on.

"My indecision shows itself the moment I awake in the morning. I start to get up; then it occurs to me that perhaps I ought not to get up immediately. So I lie down again, wondering just what I ought to do. I am beset by doubts. Not until somebody enters my room and insists on my rising can I bring myself to do so.

"At once a terrible conflict begins within me as to the clothes I should wear. Every article of my clothing has to be carefully considered. It is as if a vital problem had to be solved. Sometimes, after I am dressed, the thought strikes me that my underwear may be too light, or too heavy, or that something else is the matter with it.

"Then I have to undress and put on fresh underwear, which I minutely inspect. Or, perhaps, it is my shirt that troubles me, or the pattern of my neck-tie, or the suit I have put on.

"Always I fear that I have made a mistake in some way. Dressing consequently becomes an endless process to me. Even with help—and I nearly always have to be helped—it is two or three hours before I am finally dressed."

Consider also the case of a morbid doubter who was successfully treated by that well-known New England medical psychologist, Doctor Boris Sidis. In this case, doubting was only one of several disease symptoms. Here, somewhat abridged, is Doctor Sidis's own account of his patient's indulgence in trivial doubts:

"The patient is troubled by a form of *folie de doute*. He is not sure that the addresses on his letters are correctly written; and, no matter how many times he may read them over, he cannot feel assured that the addresses are correct. Some one else must read them and assure him that they are addressed correctly.

"When he has to write many letters, sometimes a sudden fear gets possession of him that he has interchanged the letters and put them into the wrong envelopes. He has then to tear open the envelopes and look the letters over again and again, to assure himself that they have been put by him into the right envelopes.

"Similarly, in turning out the gas jet, he must needs try it over again and again, and is often forced to get up from bed to try again whether the gas is 'really' shut off. He lights the gas, then tests the gas jet with a lighted match, to see whether the gas leaks and is 'really' completely shut off.

"In closing the door of his room, he must try the lock over and over again. He locks the door, and then unlocks it again, then locks it once more. Still, he is not sure. He then must shake it violently, so as to get the full assurance that the door has been actually and 'really' locked."[11]

This second illustrative instance brings out vividly a fact that deserves to be emphasised—the fact, namely, that, at bottom, these doubting manias are only exaggerations of a phenomenon of common occurrence. There are times when virtually everybody is tormented by doubts regarding matters that ought not to cause any indecision or perplexity. Moreover, while comparatively few people feel the need of going to a physician to be cured of abnormal doubting, there are many others who might advantageously seek the specialist's aid. People are often blind to their great weakness in this respect, though their friends may see clearly that their vacillation with regard to things great or small constitutes a defect that of itself accounts amply for their inability to make headway in the world and rise above mediocrity.

Like the Washington neurologist's patient, if in less degree, there are people to whom the choice of clothing presents a prodigious problem. To others, the choice of foods is a never-ending puzzle. At every meal they find themselves sadly at a loss to decide what they shall eat. Others, again, acting in much the fashion of the young man treated by Doctor Sidis, conjure up visions of possible mistakes and mishaps in connection with the writing and mailing of letters, the opening or shutting of doors and windows, the carrying of umbrellas, etc. Also, there are doubters of a kind well described by an observant physician:

"There are people who doubt whether their friends really think anything of them. They think that, though they treat them courteously, this may be only common politeness, and that they may really resent their wasting their time when they call on them. They hesitate to ask these people to do things for them, though, over

[11] "Studies In Psychopathology," 1907, pp. 22-23.

and over again, the friends may have shown their willingness, and, above all, by asking favours of them in turn, may have shown that they were quite willing to put themselves under obligations.

"They doubt about their charities. They wonder whether they may really not be doing more harm than good, though they have investigated the cases, or have had them investigated, and the objects of their charity may have been proved to be quite deserving. They hesitate about the acquisition of new friends, and doubt whether they should give them any confidence, and whether the confidences they have received from them are not really baits."[12]

Here, decidedly, we have a state of affairs not only breeding unhappiness, but involving a vast waste of nervous energy. This it is that chiefly makes the yielding to trivial doubts a menace to human welfare. To conserve energy for useful purposes, we are so constituted that ordinarily the little acts of everyday life—our rising, dressing, eating, attending to household or business details of a routine character—are done by us automatically. We take it for granted that we do them correctly, and, usually, we so do them. If now and then we make a mistake, we think little about it. Rightly, we regard it as of no account, compared with matters of more importance. Thus we conserve our energy for our life work. Whereas the doubter about trivialities fritters his energy away.

And, now, taking up the question of the causation of this costly habit of doubting about trivialities, let us turn once more to the cases of the two morbid doubters who consulted the Washington and Boston specialists.

In both of these cases, psychological analysis was undertaken to ascertain the causes of the exaggerated tendency to doubt. In both it was found that the patients had been subjected in childhood to conditions almost inevitably productive of a profound distrust of self. This was particularly true in the Washington case. The patient in this case was the only son of parents whose love had led them to be over-solicitous about him. When he was a little fellow they could not bear to have him out of their sight, lest something should happen to him. They had anticipated his wishes, done for him things that he might very well have done for himself; and, when he did attempt to do things for himself, they intervened to help him.

The result was an enfeebling of his consciousness and of his will. The man grew up without initiative. People had always done things for him, had always decided things for him. How could any one expect him to decide anything for himself? It was not that he was naturally weak-minded, weak-willed; it was that his training had engendered in him conditions making for mental confusion and instability of purpose.

Such was the outcome of the neurologist's psychological study of his case. It held the possibilities of a cure, through psychic re-education, having as its starting point the emancipation of this child of thirty from slavish dependence on his parents. And, in the end, after nearly two years of patient effort, a cure was actually effected.

In the second case, distrust of self had been produced in quite another way.

[12] J. J. Walsh's "Psychotherapy", p. 736.

This patient's parents had not spoiled him by over-attention. On the opposite, they had not given enough thought to the importance of developing in him emotional control, the need for which was particularly indicated in his early childhood by great dreaminess and sensitiveness of disposition. His special need for training in the control of his emotions was further evinced by the violence of his reactions to happenings of a disturbing nature. Once, for instance, when he unexpectedly met a deformed, paralysed man, he fell to the ground in a faint.

This should have been sufficient warning to his parents that they must make every effort to stiffen his character and to protect him from needless shocks. As a matter of fact, they exposed him to conditions that would have been harmful to any child. During his early years he was thrown much into the company of an old grandfather afflicted with sundry physical and mental ailments, among them the doubting mania in an extreme form. Also, he was allowed to witness the death agonies of several relatives.

All this was bound to leave a lasting imprint on his mind and his nervous system, filling him with vague fears, both as to life in general and, in particular, as to his own ability to live successfully. It was impossible for him to escape the knowledge that he did not endure the difficult and the unpleasant as well as other children did. And, with this knowledge, distrust of self, a sense of inferiority, took firm hold of him.

Nevertheless, he contrived to get along passably until he entered college. He was nervous and a little "queer," but not markedly so. When, however, ever, he found it necessary to study unusually hard for some examinations, a breakdown came. Various disease symptoms, physical and mental, developed in him, including the habit of perpetually fretting and doubting about things of small significance. In his case, that is to say, faulty training in childhood had laid the foundation for a serious psychic weakness, to the full development of which a physical condition—fatigue—had acted as the immediate cause.

In most cases of morbid doubting that have been psychologically analysed, parental mistakes have similarly become apparent. There may be—there usually is—a constitutional tendency to nervous troubles. But the parents have not appreciated this. Or, if they have appreciated it, they have failed to offset it by education especially designed to strengthen the will and inspire self-confidence, and by measures having as their end a sound physical upbuilding. Also, they have failed—and this is of the utmost importance—to externalise the personal interests, so that self-consciousness shall be at a minimum.

This does not mean, however, that the unfavourable results of the parental mistakes cannot be remedied later in life. There is reason to believe that, even in most extreme cases of morbid doubting—except the comparatively few cases where organic brain disease is responsible for the doubting—it is possible to effect a cure. As has been said, both of these patients were cured, and their cases may be regarded as fairly typical of this variety of mental affliction at its worst. Accordingly, when the tendency to trivial doubts is less marked, there is the possibility not only of cure, but of self-cure, provided that the doubter recognises exactly wherein he is deficient.

Self-consciousness, timidity, distrust of self, a conscious or subconscious feeling of inferiority, and often a lack of physical vigour—these are the elements that chiefly contribute to the growth of a tendency to anxiety and indecision about trivial things; these are the weaknesses that specially need to be overcome. As a preliminary measure, the doubter should make it a rule to take exercise daily in the open air, and to see to it that his living and sleeping quarters are kept well ventilated.

Indecision, even in the most energetic of men, is frequently a resultant of deprivation of fresh air. To reach decisions, to settle doubts quickly, a well-nourished brain is indispensable. And no brain can be well nourished unless the blood flowing to it is amply supplied with oxygen. Of all persons, therefore, the habitual doubter is in need of plenty of fresh air and of physical exercise to build up his organism as a whole and increase his powers of resistance to fatigue. For the same reason, he needs an abundance of good food.

Physical upbuilding, moreover, will have the desirable effect of increasing his power of concentrating attention on some serious life interest. This, above everything else, is what the doubter needs to do. He must develop an ardent interest in something worth while—his work, a useful hobby, occupation of some sort. The trivial doubter—the doubter of any kind—is pre-eminently a man or woman devoid of a keen life interest. If a life interest were present, there would be neither time nor inclination to dissipate energy in useless doubting. If you, my reader, recognise in yourself one of the doubting kind, you will appreciate the truth of this. You will admit that you have little enthusiasm for your work, little interest in anything that would keep you from being too occupied with thoughts of self.

Developing such an interest, self-consciousness will diminish, self-confidence will grow. Gradually, less and less attention will be paid to the petty details of daily existence that formerly gave so much concern. They will be pushed more and more into the background of the mind, will be managed automatically, as it was intended they should be managed. No longer will your indecision be a source of pitying, perhaps amused, comment by your friends. Instead, they will have occasion to comment, with pleased surprise, on the vigour and promptness of decision in all things that has taken the place of the old indecision.

One word more:

Exactly as hygienic measures are helpful in the cure of indecision in adults, so are they helpful to prevent the development of indecision—and bashfulness—in children. Parents will do well to bear this in mind. But, as in the prevention of selfishness, jealousy, and so forth, reliance on hygienic measures alone is not enough. It is all very well to see that children get plenty of good food, abundant muscular exercise, and much life in the open air. This is excellent and necessary. Also, however, they must be given wise moral training—training that will make it habitual for them to think and act vigourously, to keep their emotions well in hand, to be interested in much besides themselves, and to develop the feeling of self-confidence and the spirit of initiative.

Now, let us turn to still another preventable and serious life handicap having its origin in the days of childhood—the handicap of stammering.

CHAPTER VII

STAMMERING

THERE lies convenient to my hand at this moment a thin, pamphlet-like volume that tells the story of one of the strangest, among the many singular and tragic blunders which medical science has made in its progress to knowledge. It is a translation from the German of Doctor J. F. Dieffenbach's "Memoir on the Radical Cure of Stuttering." Assuredly, Dieffenbach's "cure" was radical enough, for it consisted in nothing less than the excision of a large, wedge-shaped section from the stammerer's tongue! In this little book, published in 1841, and embellished with several ghastly full-page engravings, is described, with great professional gusto, the first of these terrible operations as performed, without the merciful aid of any anesthetic, on an unhappy boy of thirteen. The result was a "complete success." Says Dieffenbach, writing a few weeks after the operation:

"At the present time not the slightest trace of stuttering remains, not the slightest vibration of the muscles of the face, not the most inconsiderable play of the lips. His speech is, throughout, well toned, even, and flowing."

Thus was inaugurated a period of butchery that lasted until—almost before the year was out—it was observed that those "cured" by this sanguinary means usually began, before long, to stammer as badly as ever, and also that those who were not "cured" had a tendency to die. Yet Dieffenbach was no charlatan, no "quack." He was a reputable surgeon who honestly believed that he had discovered the true remedy for stammering. And, if the passage of time has intensified the tragedy and absurdity of his method and has relegated his glowing account of it to a place in the literature of medical curiosities, there is this to be said of him—that he has had plenty of successors who have erred almost as seriously in their attempts to solve the problem presented by the widespread and baffling malady of stammering.

In fact, up to within quite recent times the record of the struggle against stammering has been one of continuous failure. There has been a steady accumulation of methods of treatment, from surgical operations of a less drastic type than Dieffenbach's to the use of various articulatory and respiratory exercises and devices, without any appreciable effect in the diminution of stammering. Even to-day the great majority of physicians and lay specialists—to whom, by a sort of tacit agreement, the medical profession has largely relinquished the task of dealing with stammering—labour to next to no purpose. At this very moment there are in the United States at least three hundred thousand persons who stammer, fully half of whom stammer so badly that they are severely handicapped in the gaining of a livelihood. Thousands of these have resorted to medical advice, or have attended so-called schools for stammerers, with lastingly beneficial results to few. Small wonder that there is, among stammerers and their friends, a tendency to believe that stammering is one of the hopelessly incurable maladies of mankind.

And this would undeniably appear to be true, as regards many stammerers. On the other hand, it may confidently be said that nearly all cases of stammering are actually susceptible of marked improvement, often amounting to 75 or 90 per cent. of a cure; and that a number of cases can be completely cured. Such a statement, to be sure, could not have been safely made even a few years ago. This for the reason that only lately has there been any really systematic effort by scientifically trained investigators to study the phenomena of stammering, with a view to ascertaining, with scientific exactness, its true nature and causation.

Stammering, it has long been recognised, is not a malady of uniform symptomatology, like tuberculosis or typhoid fever. No two stammerers stammer precisely alike. They stumble over different letters and sounds; time, place, and circumstances have varying effects on the degree of their stammering; and the physical spasms and contortions that so often accompany this trouble differ in different stammerers. There is, too, a great variation in the onset of stammering. Mostly, it is true, it manifests itself in childhood, from the age of four to eleven. But it may not set in until much later in life; and, when it does begin in childhood, it begins under much diversity of conditions.

Sometimes a child stammers almost as soon as he has learned to speak, though seldom, if ever, coincident with the learning. Often, the first appearance of stammering follows some disease like measles or diphtheria. Or, again, a child who has been speaking quite well, suddenly begins to stammer, and persists in stammering, after being brought into contact with people who are themselves stammerers.

"I was entirely free of stammering," declares a clergyman, in a typical statement, "till I was five years old. At that time of life there was a gentleman who occasionally came to my father's house, and stammered very badly. I distinctly remember one afternoon trying to imitate him; when, unfortunately, he heard me, and was very indignant. So ashamed were my parents at my conduct that, after he had gone, I was taken to task and punished severely for it. Ever since that night I have been afflicted with this most distressing malady, in spite of all my efforts to overcome it."

Compare a statement by a Philadelphia physician, Doctor D. Braden Kyle:

"Several years ago I saw three interesting cases of stammering. Two of the cases were imitation. These two lads, who were associated with a boy several years older, the worst stammerer I ever saw, clearly imitated him. As they were constantly together, the imitation was almost continuous. They certainly developed into expert stammerers. In less than two years they were confirmed stammerers, and it was impossible for them to speak at all without stuttering and stammering."

Facts like these, I repeat, have long been observed and commented on by specialists in the treatment of stammering; but they have, for the most part, been dismissed as mere "oddities," while emphasis has been laid on the single fact that, in the majority of cases, stammerers have had parents or other relatives who themselves stammered. "Heredity," consequently, has been assumed to be the one and sufficient explanation of all stammering; and it has also been assumed that what is inherited is either an anatomical or a physiological defect. Hence, in too many instances, the use of the surgeon's knife; and, hence, the invention of innumerable systems designed to train the stammerer in the correct use of his breathing and articulating organs—in a word, systems intended to teach him how to talk.

But, as even the most enthusiastic exponents of these corrective systems are now beginning to appreciate, whatever else the stammerer may need, he does not need to be taught how to talk. For he can talk well enough on occasion. Nothing is more significant, from the standpoint of assisting to a clear understanding of the nature of stammering, than the fact that there are uncommonly few stammerers who have any difficulty in speaking when nobody is with them. On this point, every stammerer with whom I have been in touch is in remarkable agreement, and others who have had a far wider acquaintance with stammerers testify to the same effect. For example, Mr. Charles L. Rowan, of Milwaukee, a gentleman who has stammered for years and has made a close study of the subject, informs me:

"When I am alone—and the same is true of other stammerers—I have no speech difficulty whatever, and can talk or read aloud for hours with ease. It is only when I am with others that I halt and stammer in my speech. Sometimes I talk in my sleep, and the folks tell me I do not stammer then. But, if I am dreaming, and in the dream imagine myself talking, it is always in a stammer.

"I have also noticed that most stammerers talk better when the subject is light and frivolous than when it is something serious. And they talk better when conversing with people whom they regard as inferiors. I know a man who is a section foreman, and he says he can give orders to his negro and Mexican labourers perfectly, but if the roadmaster comes along he cannot talk to him at all."

And a stammerer from Spokane, Washington, informs me:

"I would like to say that there are periods when I can talk much better than for corresponding periods. Indeed, there are times, generally a few days at a time, when it is most difficult for me to talk with even a slight degree of correctness; and, then, there are periods of as long, or longer, duration when speech seems to flow with more ease, though never perfect, except for a few words in succession."

More than this, according to one diligent investigator, the majority of stammerers fail to stammer if addressed in such a way that their replies are made without their realising that they are talking. Says this observer:

"Suppose a stammerer is engaged in a deep study and unaware of your presence. You speak to him softly. He answers readily, without hesitation, in an absent manner. Again, you ask a careless question, implying by your manner that you do not expect or desire an answer; to this he quickly and easily replies also. Now, look straight at him and pointedly interrogate him. See, when it becomes necessary for him to speak, how he is thrown into confusion."

It has further been found that most stammerers are at their worst when in the presence of strangers. Some stammer scarcely at all when at home with their relatives and intimate friends. On the opposite, there are some who stammer worse than usual when with relatives. Not so long ago I learned of one stammerer—a young lady who had stammered from early childhood—whose trouble was most in evidence when she was talking with her mother. Almost all stammerers, too, enjoy temporary relief from their speech defect when greatly startled, angry, or otherwise excited.

Decidedly, then, it is not from anatomical or physiological inability to speak that a stammerer suffers. It is, rather, from a psychological inability. That is to say, the facts just mentioned indicate strongly that stammering is primarily a mental malady—that it is due to the presence, in the mind of the stammerer, of some idea or ideas that inhibit the normal functioning of the organs of speech. This conclusion is confirmed by the additional circumstance that nearly every stammerer who has been questioned on the subject admits that he is perpetually tormented by a haunting dread of not being able to express himself clearly to others, and so of exposing himself to their ridicule, contempt, or pity. Many, indeed, affirm their conviction that if they could only overcome this dread they would be free from their affliction. "I believe," is a characteristic utterance of stammerers, "that if I were to wake up some morning with total forgetfulness that I had ever stammered, I should never stammer again."

Still more significant is the fact that, of the many methods which have been invented for the treatment of stammering—and which include such curious devices as beating time with every word, and wearing artificial supports under the tongue—all have had to their credit a certain—however small—proportion of genuine cures. This would suggest, not that they have been intrinsically valuable, but that, in the cases cured, they so impressed the mind of the stammerer with their therapeutic virtue as to banish his long-entertained belief that he could not talk like other people. For that matter, recent experiments go to bear out the view that almost any method, no matter how fantastic, will cure some stammerers, if only they have a lively faith in its efficacy.

For example, there was once brought to the Boston City Hospital a woman of thirty-five, who, though formerly speaking without any difficulty, had begun to stammer in a frightful manner, following a violent quarrel with her husband. She could utter scarcely a sound, except weirdly inarticulate noises, and these only by a great effort. The physician to whom her case was entrusted soon became satisfied that she was suffering mainly from a profound belief that she would never be able to talk again; and he therefore endeavoured to reason her out of this, but to no purpose. Finally, he abandoned the attempt, and, after leaving her pretty much to her own devices for several days, impressively said to her one morning, in a tone of great authority:

"Well, Mrs. Blank, I have been looking carefully into your case, and I find there is one way certain to cure you. It may be a little painful, but I know you will not mind that, as long as it is going to make you entirely well."

So saying, and with an air of the utmost confidence, he began to apply to her an electric current, just strong enough to make her wince. Only a few treatments of this sort were found necessary to enable the hospital authorities to discharge her as cured—and she stayed cured.

Of late, consequently, with growing recognition of the dominant psychic factor in stammering, there has been an increasing tendency—though as yet it is far from universal—to employ psychological methods in treating stammerers. The effort is made to instil confidence in the sufferer—to convince him that he need only exercise his will power to bring about his own cure. In a good many cases, and frequently with gratifying results, resort is had to hypnotism, the "suggestion" being reiterated to the patient, while in the hypnotic state, that in the future he will experience none of his overwhelming sensations of dread and anxiety and will speak as fluently as persons who have never stammered. Or he may be treated by psychic re-education, which consists essentially in the development of volitional control by suggestions tactfully imparted in the ordinary waking state. All of which unquestionably marks a tremendous advance over the theories and practices based on the alleged anatomical or physiological defects of stammerers.

There is this to be added, though, that, sanely beneficial as is the psychological treatment of stammering, it often happens that the confidence-inspiring suggestions given to stammerers do not "take." The stammerer, albeit he may perhaps show improvement for a time, remains without clear articulatory power. When this occurs, the natural tendency among those treating him—in view of the demonstrated truth that stammering is the effect of a peculiar state of mind—is to throw the blame on the patient instead of on the method. Yet, actually, it is the method that is at fault—or, to be exact, it is the failure to apply the method, which itself is thoroughly sound—in such a way as to remove from the stammerer's mind not only the fear that haunts him and helps to perpetuate his stammering, *but also the ideas in which his stammering originated.*

Here we come to the central fact in the whole problem of stammering—a fact which, when it is widely enough known and appreciated, is certain to exert a far-reaching influence on the prevention of stammering, as well as its cure. Until very recently, few have been aware of this fact except a small group of foreign investigators, physicians with a psychological training, whose special business it has been to determine scientifically the possibilities, the limitations, and the exact procedures to be followed in supplementing, by wholly mental treatment, the ordinary medical and surgical treatment of disease. Impressed by the predominance of the mental factor in stammering, these investigators were particularly impressed by some of the peculiarities mentioned above—as, the ability of almost every stammerer to speak well when alone or when in a state of abstraction. Such peculiarities, they knew from long experience, bore a strong resemblance to oddities in the behaviour of victims of hysteria, psychasthenia, or other psychoneurosis, in all of which disorders there is a tendency for symptoms to disappear when the sufferer's attention is momentarily withdrawn from them. Accordingly, it seemed to the investigators quite possible that, in the last analysis, stammering was not so much a disease in itself as a psychoneurotic symptom.

They were well aware, for reasons already set forth in these pages, that psychoneurotic disorders have their origin in emotional disturbances of one sort or another, which, occurring to a person of nervous temperament or rendered neurally unstable by a faulty upbringing, react adversely on the entire organism. Exactly what happens is that the emotional disturbance—whether it be a fright, a grief, a worry, or what not—while perhaps completely forgotten by the victim, so far as conscious recollection is concerned, remains subconsciously alive in his memory, is ever seeking to emerge again into conscious remembrance, and, failing to do this, takes its revenge, so to speak, by the production of disease symptoms ranging from mere eccentricities of thought and behaviour to symptoms mimicking those of true organic disease.

Also, the investigators knew that the particular form these mentally caused symptoms take depends chiefly on the kind of suggestions received from the sufferer's environment. If he chances, for instance, to have a relative or a friend who is a paralytic, he may, in time, develop pseudosymptoms of paralysis himself. Or, if his nervous equilibrium be sufficiently upset, he may develop them from merely hearing or reading about them. Whatever the symptoms he manifests, his malady is curable—precisely as it was produced—by mental means alone. Often, a counter-suggestion, to the effect that henceforth the psychoneurotic person will be perfectly well, is enough to work his cure. Or, permanently curative effects may be had only when, by special techniques devised for the express purpose of rummaging through the subconsciousness, the forgotten memory, or memories, responsible for the psychoneurosis are brought to light, and the specific suggestion directly or indirectly made that from that time they will do no harm. Sometimes, experience has shown, the mere recalling of them to conscious remembrance is enough to put an end to the disease symptoms they have caused.

On the view that stammering is similarly a psychoneurotic symptom, and that, when it fails to yield to treatment by general suggestion, it is because the subconscious memories underlying it are too intense to be thus subdued, this group of investigators undertook to treat it as they would any stubborn psychoneurosis. The outcome of their experiments has been such that I feel justified in declaring that science has at last penetrated to the true inwardness of stammering. These psychologically trained physicians have taken stammerers who had well-nigh exhausted their hopes and their resources in a futile quest for normal speech, and, after subjecting them to the searching methods of psychological analysis, have sent them on their way rejoicing, either in a perfect cure or in a lasting improvement far beyond their expectation.

Citing a few instances of actual occurrence, a German member of the group, Doctor B. Dattner, was once consulted by a stammerer of thirty-six, who had been burdened by his speech defect from boyhood. He had first stammered, he told Doctor Dattner, after an attack of diphtheria, at the age of nine; and he had for some time been treated on the supposition that the diphtheria had caused a peculiar kind of throat paralysis.[13] This treatment failing, he had sought relief by

[13] It is important to recognise that certain organic diseases of the central nervous system do sometimes, through destructive action on the lower speech centres, cause incurable

other means, always without more than temporary benefit. Like many another stammerer, he spoke of the abnormal dread that harassed him, especially when with strangers, and expressed the belief that if he could conquer this he would be free from his stammer.

"Ah, but," Doctor Dattner pointed out, "do you not realise that, after all, your dread is caused by—not the cause of—your stammer? It has helped, doubtless, to keep it alive and to aggravate it. But it has not been the thing that originally made you stammer. That we must seek elsewhere."

"You mean in the attack of diphtheria?"

"Not at all. I mean in something that happened to you before you had diphtheria—something which so exceedingly distressed you that it was continually uppermost in your thoughts, and which finally worked on you so much that when your nervous system was weakened by the diphtheria it gave rise to your stammering. Now, we are going to try to discover what that something was, and, when we have done so, it will be possible really to cure you. Can you recall any particularly disagreeable incident of your childhood occurring at any time before you were ill of diphtheria?"

"No," said the other, after a little reflection, "I think that I was perfectly happy as a child, and certainly I was treated kindly."

"Just the same, something must have happened at that period to disturb you very much. Let us find out, if we can, what it was."

To this end, Doctor Dattner now made use of the "free association method of mental analysis," which consists in requesting the patient to concentrate his attention on his symptoms, and state without reserve the thoughts coming to him in connection with them—the theory being that, if there is any exceptionally distressing idea underlying them, the current of his spoken thoughts will, soon or late, reveal it. In the present instance, this method at first brought forth only trivial and commonplace memory associations. But, after a time, a reminiscence of intense emotional colouring suddenly emerged.

It related to an episode of the stammerer's eighth year, shortly before his attack of diphtheria, when he was pounced upon and frightened almost into convulsions by a huge black dog. This had virtually faded from his conscious memory; but now, as he sat in the quiescent mood enjoined on all patients undergoing psychoanalytic treatment, it welled up into full recollection, every detail of it being vividly recalled—the sight of the dog, the emotions of fear and horror, the hysterical shrieking that followed his escape, the difficulty his parents had in convincing him that he was unharmed. He used to lie awake, he remembered, thinking of the dog; he used to dream of it; the thought of it was always with him.

"Precisely," said Doctor Dattner, drily. "And, you see, the thought of it is still with you, for look how graphically you have described it all. The trouble is that it

speech defect resembling stammering. Thus, a "stammerer" whom I referred to Doctor Coriat was found to be a victim, not of true stammering, but of the effects of a paralysis-causing organic disease experienced in early life. This condition, however, is of infrequent occurrence; and its presence can be readily determined by a neurologist.

has been leading an independent existence, as it were, in the depths of your mind, with all its original emotional intensity. Your stammering, I can assure you, has been nothing more than the external manifestation, the symbol, of its continuing presence, and of the deadly power it has had over you—sensitive, impressionable child that you must have been. But I can also assure you that your stammering will now come to an end; for we have not only found its cause in the subconsciously remembered shock of your boyhood, but we have actually removed that cause by the very fact of recalling it to your conscious recollection and, consequently, finding a normal outlet for the repressed emotions."

Altogether, it had required just six hours of psychoanalysis, at the rate of about an hour a day, to recover this horror-encrusted memory of the stammerer's childhood. But, with its recall, and strikingly validating Doctor Dattner's confident prediction, he once more began to enjoy the blessing of a facile, flowing speech.

In another case—treated by the American neurologist, Doctor Coriat, who has made extensive use of psychoanalytic methods—the patient was a man of middle age, who stammered not only when he spoke, but even when he wrote, repeating letters and syllables in anything he tried to put on paper. He had been to two stammering schools and had been discharged from both as cured, but each time had speedily relapsed.

As in the case of Doctor Dattner's patient, psychoanalysis demonstrated that the causal agency of his stammering was a lingering subconscious remnant of distressing emotional states experienced in childhood. Only, in this instance, the distressing states related, not to an unexpected, stupefying fright, but to painful reveries indulged in as a child, and occasioned by certain unpleasant stories he had been told regarding the end of the world and the fate of the sinful.

"These," he recalled, "took complete possession of my mind. I became convinced that the end of the world could not be long delayed, and I was in an agony of terror. Constantly I kept asking myself what I should do to escape destruction. I knew I was a bad boy—very bad. Nothing could atone for the sins I fancied I had committed. But I kept my fears to myself; I did not dare confide them to others. Night and day I worried about them, picturing to myself the terrible happenings of the approaching time of doom."

Until psychoanalysis brought them up to the surface of consciousness, he had long ceased to think of these foolish imaginings of childhood. He had as entirely forgotten them as though he had never entertained them. But, as the event showed, it was their malign influence, working on a nervous system already infirm by defects of inheritance, that had produced a psychoneurosis which, in his case, had taken the form of a speech disorder through the suggestions unconsciously absorbed by watching his mother, who likewise suffered from a peculiar variety of stammering.

Another of Doctor Coriat's patients—a young woman—impressed him, from the day of her first visit, with her extreme timidity and self-consciousness. Both were so pronounced as to be abnormal, and he immediately suspected that they, in common with her stammering, would be found linked with subconscious memories of occurrences that had tended to deprive her of proper appreciation of her abilities and rights. She proved a good hypnotic subject, and, knowing that in hypnosis long-forgotten events are easily recalled, Doctor Coriat questioned her as to her previous history.

"Can you remember," he asked her, "just when it was that you began to stammer?"

"It was when I was a very little girl."

"Had any one or anything greatly frightened you before then?"

"Yes."

"What was it?"

"It was my father."

Then followed, in answer to further questions, a long series of reminiscences of the severe discipline imposed on her in earliest childhood by her father, a stern, hard man. As she related them, she seemed to feel again all the emotions that they had provoked—the shame, grief, fear, doubt, longing for sympathy. Literally, she lived through them anew, and to the trained understanding of the physician it was evident that she had never really forgotten them—although, in the waking state, she was able to recall her childhood only vaguely—but had subconsciously dwelt on them all her life, to the wrecking of her self-confidence, as well as the causing of her troubles of speech. Only by completely blotting them out, through psychotherapeutic means, could her restoration to health be effected.

Similarly, it has been found that emotional disturbances are at the bottom of stammering when it develops, not in childhood, but in adult life. A particularly instructive case, because of the insight it affords into the ingenuity with which the expert psychoanalyst gets at the truth in even the most complicated cases of functional nervous or mental disorder, is one that was successfully handled by Doctor A. A. Brill, already mentioned in these pages, a pupil of the pioneer Austrian psychoanalyst, Doctor Sigmund Freud. Doctor Brill's patient was a man who, after an early life untroubled by speech defect, had begun to stammer from no discernible cause, and had been stammering for a number of years before he consulted the New York specialist. Several weeks of psychoanalysis elicited nothing that would account for his trouble, and Doctor Brill was in much perplexity, until he one day noticed that the words on which his patient chiefly stammered were words beginning with or containing the letter "k." It occurred to him that this letter might have some significant association in the stammerer's mind, but the latter denied that it could have.

However, after psychoanalysis had proceeded further, Doctor Brill learned that there had been an event in the patient's life, though occurring some little time before the development of the stammering, that had made a most painful, even agonising, impression on him. He had been engaged to a young woman who had eloped with his closest friend; and this had so wrought on him that he had vowed never to utter her name again.

"And what was her name?" asked Doctor Brill.

The stammerer stared at him and burst into a violent tirade.

"Haven't I just told you," he cried, "that I have taken an oath never to speak it? What business is it of yours, anyway? What bearing can it have on my trouble of speech?"

"Only this bearing—that it may be the means of curing you. Come, now, I am sorry you have taken an oath, because you will have to break it and tell me the name."

"I'll die first."

With this he seized his hat and dashed out of the doctor's office in a frenzy of indignation. Doctor Brill did not see him again for a month. Then he returned, repentant. He would tell the name, he said, on condition that Doctor Brill did not write it down in the detailed record which, as is customary, he was making of the case. To this a prompt assent was given, and the troublesome name was as promptly made known. As Doctor Brill had expected, it began with K. He then said, leaning forward and showing his sheet of notes:

"See, I have kept my promise. I have called her Miss W. And, now, we'll soon have you quite well."

But on his next visit the patient was in despair. He was, he protested, stammering worse than ever. Words that had never given him any trouble before were now almost unpronounceable by him. On investigation, it turned out that they were, one and all, words in which the letter "w" had a place.

"At last," said Doctor Brill, "we know for a certainty what has made you stammer. It was the foolish oath you took, which served to sustain in your mind the memory of the terrible experience you went through on account of your faithless sweetheart. Vowing never to utter her name, yet thinking constantly of her, you have unconsciously made it difficult for you to utter even words in which the most prominent letter of that name—its initial—occurs. And, now, since she has become Miss W. to you, as well as Miss K., you are stammering on words with "w," as well as words with "k." We must free you from the torment of that vow and of the pent-up emotions that go with the forbidden name, and then you will never stammer more."

To this mode of dealing with stammerers could anything be in stronger contrast than the brutal Dieffenbach technique? The latter exemplifies, if in an extreme form, the folly of attempting—as is so often done, even to-day—to treat stammering on a basis of imperfect observation. The former shows the happy results that may be obtained when it is attacked in the light of thorough investigation. No; it is neither by the surgeon's knife nor by the use of mechanical appliances or physiological devices that stammering is to be really conquered, but by intelligent application of the wonderful remedial measures which modern medical psychology has worked out.

Stammering, to recapitulate, is not at bottom an anatomical or physiological trouble. Its individual peculiarities, varied as they are, all tend to prove that it is a mental malady, symptomatic of a psychoneurosis having its origin in subconscious emotional states. The rôle that heredity plays in it is merely to provide the soil in which it can flourish. Of wholly mental causation, it is curable by mental means, whether by faith in the efficacy of any method of treatment, however intrinsically worthless that method may be; by "suggestions" of a general character; or, if needful, by specific recall and eradication of the "forgotten memories" that underlie it.

Lest, however, I raise hope unduly, I would at once add that not even the most expert practitioners in psychoanalysis, or in any other psychological mode of treating stammering, are justified in guaranteeing an absolute or an "approximate" cure in every case. Experience is showing that the "emotional complexes" responsible for stammering are, in many cases, so deep-seated—and often so entangled in later complexes—that it is virtually impossible to get at them by any present-known method of mind tunnelling. And, in many other cases, the process of psychoanalysis is so slow and tedious that the stammerer is all too likely to lose heart and abandon the effort at cure.

Consequently, in respect to stammering, prevention becomes of more than usual importance. And the prevention of stammering, I trust I have already made amply clear, rests chiefly with parents. It is again primarily a question of guarding the young from needless emotional stresses, of early training to foster in children calmness, courage, self-confidence; so that, when inevitable shocks and trials come, they will have no power to overwhelm the mind and give birth to stammering or any other neurotic evil.

CHAPTER VIII

FAIRY TALES THAT HANDICAP

"EVERY ugly thing told to the child, every shock, every fright given him, will remain like minute splinters in the flesh to torture him all his life long."

Thus said the famous Italian scientist, Angelo Mosso, a good many years ago. The facts of more recent research into the psychology and psychopathology of childhood, as reviewed in the preceding chapters, vindicate Professor Mosso's statement to an extent and in ways undreamed of by him. Nor is it only the emotionally disturbing things seen, heard, or experienced by children that may have a decisively adverse influence on their development. Harm may similarly and equally be done by the books and stories they read, even to the extent of provoking or accentuating nervous maladies. Particularly mischievous in this respect, because of their wide reading by children, are certain fairy tales which many parents—nay, I might say, nearly all parents—consider quite suitable for young readers.

You smile incredulously at the suggestion that a fairy tale could possibly affect a child harmfully. Still more preposterous seems to you the idea that the harmful effects of fairy tales—if such harmful effects actually occur—may be carried over into adult life. But, listen:

To the Doctor Brill of the letter "k" stammering case just narrated, there once came a young man of twenty-eight, afflicted with a strange and alarming malady.

"Doctor," he said, "I want your candid opinion as to what is the matter with me. Physically I feel well, but mentally I am badly off. In fact, I fear I am insane, and dangerously so. For a long time I have been tormented by a strange desire to bite and stab people and to torture them in all sorts of ways. I yearn for the times when everybody carried the dirk and dagger and could kill when offended. As yet I have restrained my mad impulse, but I am in terror lest I give way to it. Is there anything you can do to help me?"

The mere fact that he thus clearly recognised and candidly confessed his mental state was in itself a hopeful sign. But Doctor Brill was well aware that it might be extremely difficult to cure him, perhaps impossible. Everything would depend, in the first place, on whether the young man were actually insane or merely the victim of a psychoneurotic obsession. If the latter, there was a possibility of his being cured, provided the subconscious region of his mind could be explored with sufficient thoroughness to get at and root out the ideas underlying and responsible for his dangerous obsession. Satisfying himself that it actually was a case of psychoneurosis, Doctor Brill began the work of mental exploration. And, knowing that submerged ideas are pretty sure to reveal themselves, directly or indirectly, through the character of a person's dreams, he began by directing the young man to make a written record of his dreaming.

"Whenever you have a dream," he told him, "I want you to write it down as soon as you awake, and bring me an account of it."

Before long, Doctor Brill was in possession of a remarkable collection of dreams, many of which, as he had expected, were of an exceedingly unpleasant character. Analysing these dreams, a curious fact at once became evident—namely, that the patient's mental life was largely occupied with imaginings that related, not to the world of everyday existence, but to the people and events of mythology and fairy tale.

Always, too, in his subconscious imaginings, ideas of death and violence were uppermost. During the dream-analysis he recalled with special vividness such themes as the beheading of Medusa, the cruelties of Bluebeard, and the freezing to death of Eva, heroine of Bryant's "Little People of the Snows." Even trivial details in the settings of these and similar fairy tales were remembered and brought out in his dream-associations with a fulness that astonished the patient himself. Dr. Brill comments:

"He was very imaginative, so that the harrowing adventures enacted by fairies, genii, and Greek deities, on which he was constantly fed, were deeply interwoven with his own life, and he built up for himself a strange, archaic world. He liked to be alone, and often wandered away from his companions, to act through, in his own way, the adventures of which he had just heard or read.

"He himself traced the selection of his profession—that of an actor—to these boyish actions when he tried to imitate the fleet-footed Mercury, some character from fairyland or the "Arabian Nights," or some savage Indians. He thus imagined himself flying, and beheading monsters above the clouds, or penetrating to the centre of the earth in the form of some wicked magician, all the time passing through the most harrowing scenes. By a process of condensation, he fused ancient characters and episodes with persons and actions of reality, but his fancies usually began with some god-like or demon-like myth and gradually descended to human beings.

"During the first few weeks of the analysis he was in the habit of merging into a dreamy state while reproducing associations, and often became so excited that the work had to be temporarily interrupted."[14]

It was unnecessary to seek much further for the explanation of the obsession of torture. In large part, at all events, this was quite evidently the expression in consciousness of the gruesome images with which the patient's mind had been filled by the tales told him in his childhood. Though faded from conscious remembrance, they had remained with him subconsciously, to influence for evil the current of his conscious thoughts. Or, to put the matter tersely: Had tales of cruelty and violent death not been told him in his early days, he might never have been afflicted in manhood with his morbid longings to inflict pain.

[14] *The New York Medical Journal,* March 21, 1914.

Of course, if this case stood by itself it would be of no great significance. But the fact is that during the past few years—or since physicians began to appreciate the part played by childhood impressions in causing mental and nervous disease—evidence has been accumulating to indicate that the almost universal custom of telling fairy tales to children does entail grave risks to their character and their health. The child of normal nervous constitution is likely to be affected only in character; the supersensitive, neurotic child may be hurried, by the tales he hears or reads, into some more or less serious mental or nervous malady.

Let me hasten to add that this does not mean that the fairy tale should be entirely banished from the literature of childhood. It means only that parents should exercise more discrimination than they usually show in selecting fairy tales for their children. The rightly chosen fairy tale is indeed an almost indispensable aid in the early education of children, for reasons that are admirably summarised by an American educator, Mr. Percival Chubb, in these words:

"One value in fairy stories for the young is that they embody and commemorate the man-child's first rude assertion of the lordship of mind, and subserve the development of a later sense of spiritual freedom and autonomy. Another is that they are expressive, as all art is expressive, of the idealistic hunger at the heart of men. Again, as forms of art, they select and co-ordinate those facts which bring out the spiritual meanings of life. That is, they release from the unsifted materials of experience the imprisoned 'Soul of Fact.' And not only do they embody the basic moral insights and interpretations of childish man, but they express the simple and larger emotions, and so feed the heart of the child. They quicken, too, the imagination—that master-faculty without which the sympathy which is man's highest and richest endowment fails of fruition. They are an aid to culture by giving an outlook upon all nations and kindreds, all countries and conditions of life. Finally, along with their allied forms of literary invention, the myth, saga, fable, and so on, they are a condition to understanding the innumerable allusions with which the literature of the world is studded."[15]

All this is assuredly the function of the fairy tale, but frequently it is frustrated by the kind of fairy tales children are allowed to read. For one thing, the imaginative faculty is scarcely stimulated in a healthy fashion when the mind is led to dwell constantly, as in the case of Doctor Brill's patient, on thoughts of cruelty and pain. Nor can the fairy tale be said to have exerted a healthy influence in such a case as that represented by a little girl who was brought for treatment to another medical psychologist, and whose morbid irritability, disobedience, and crying spells were, by psychological analysis, traced to an excessive jealousy of her brother. In the course of the analysis the discovery was made that the girl had frequent dreams of seeing both her mother and her brother cruelly treated. In one dream, witches shut her mother in a cave to starve to death, and threw her brother into a large caldron of boiling water, leaving her to perish miserably.

"This dream," the little girl naïvely explained to the physician who was analysing her mental states, "is just like the fairy tales I read."

[15] Proceedings of the National Education Association, 1905, p. 871 *et seq.*

Other dreams of cruelty were likewise found to be drawn from the reading of unpleasant fairy tales. So that, although in this case jealousy was undoubtedly the chief cause of the nervous condition for which treatment was required, fairy tales also played a part in directing the course of the little girl's morbid thinking and her difficult behaviour. Warned by this revelation of the dream-analysis, her physician made it a point to notify her mother that unless steps were taken to change the girl's reading matter she might develop traits of character—harshness, coldness, indifference to the sufferings of others—that would handicap her throughout life.

Or, instead of causing an abnormal harshness, the fairy tale abounding in gory elements may breed an equally abnormal timidity, passing sometimes beyond the category of a character defect to that of positive disease. A typical instance is found in the experience of a young New York boy.

"Our son," his parents told the physician, to whom they took him for treatment, "has suddenly become excitable and nervous, afraid to go outdoors alone, and still more afraid to sleep alone. If left to himself after having been put to bed, he often wakes out of a sound sleep, shrieking for us. When we go to him he seems dazed, and for some moments does not recognise us. But he cannot tell us what has frightened him, and in the morning does not remember his alarm."

From this brief description the physician at once recognised that he had to deal with a case of what is technically known as *pavor nocturnus*, but better known to the lay public as "night terrors." Having had a thorough training in medical psychology, he was well aware that night terrors are grounded in disturbing experiences of the waking life. Accordingly, he questioned the parents closely.

Insistently they denied that anything had occurred to cause their son undue anxiety or alarm. Then the physician resorted to psychological analysis of the boy's mental states and, before long, made the discovery that his mind was full of frightful images of giants, wizards, and slimy monsters. Promptly he summoned the father and mother to a conference, and asked them:

"Have you been reading or telling fairy stories to your boy lately?"

"Why, yes," the mother replied. "He is passionately fond of them, and I tell him some every day."

"And what, may I ask, are the stories that you tell to him most frequently?"

"'Jack the Giant Killer' is one. He is also particularly fond of 'The Boy Who Did Not Know How to Shiver.'"

"Well, madam," said the physician, gravely, "I must ask you either to stop telling him fairy tales or to choose for him fairy tales with less gruesome elements in them. He is a boy of nervous temperament, and, figuratively speaking, he has been poisoned by the fear-images that are so abundant in the stories he has heard. Take him out into the open air, turn his thoughts to other things, and be more discreet in your choice of reading matter for him. Unless you do this, there is danger that he will yet suffer from something far more serious than night terrors."

The truth of this last statement may be concretely re-enforced by another citation from recent medical experience—the case, not of a young boy, but of a man of thirty, who came to Doctor Brill with a remarkable story.

"Ever since my boyhood," he related, "I have fainted at seeing blood. Now I feel weak and dizzy, and sometimes I faint outright, at anything which merely brings into my mind the thought of blood. I am afraid to talk to certain people because they are likely to speak about accidents which make me think of blood. The sight of a man who looks like a doctor suggests an operation, and at once I feel faint. On one occasion I fainted away while my blood pressure was being taken. It was not that I was afraid of having my blood pressure taken; it was simply that the word 'blood' brought on the usual attack. You do not appreciate the difficulty I have in telling you all this. Every time I mention the word to you I have to get a grip on myself. I fear I must seem very weak and foolish, but I cannot overcome the horror I feel. Unless you help me, I do not know what I shall do. I cannot go on this way indefinitely."

In answer to Doctor Brill's questions, he insisted nothing had occurred in his life that could give rise to his "phobia," or morbid dread of blood. He had been in no bad accident, had undergone no serious surgical operation, had witnessed no sanguinary scenes of any sort.

"Nevertheless," Doctor Brill assured him, "there is a logical reason for your abnormal fear. It is evidently buried deep in your mind; but there are ways of getting at it, and get at it we must."

Psychological analysis, patiently carried on for many days, ultimately brought the truth to light. His phobia, it appeared, had its real starting point in early childhood, and, not least, in certain sensational fairy stories read to him by a nurse when he was quite young—stories which he himself continued to read at a later age.

"These bloody and horrible stories," to quote Doctor Brill, "made a strong impression upon him. He would form fancies about them on going to sleep at night, substituting himself for the hero."

"Bluebeard" was one story that especially impressed him. Another was a charming tale about a false princess who was rolled in a barrel, into which long pointed spikes had been driven.

As he grew older, there had been the usual fading from memory of these stories and the imaginings to which they had given rise. But, subconsciously, they had never been forgotten, and out of them there had gradually developed the obsessive and seemingly inexplicable dread of blood.

In another case, the "Bluebeard" story responsible for the night terrors of a sensitive little girl, remained so indelibly fixed in her subconsciousness that in adult life she often had nightmares, in which, to her great distress, she was attacked by men who were "frightful looking on account of their blue beards." Even more impressively illustrative of the permanence and possible ill effects of tales of the horrible heard in early life is the case of a man fifty years old, who had to receive medical treatment because he "could not fall asleep without living through—for at least an hour, sometimes even longer—some distorted story from fairy books or mythology."

That common phobia of childhood, fear of the dark, is often traceable to fairy tales, and, in many cases, persists in some degree through later life. Let me quote, on this important point, the testimony of a Washington physician, Doctor T. A. Williams, who has made a special study of nervousness in childhood:

"Morbid fears are a great distress to many people. They have nearly always arisen in early childhood, and have been inculcated by injudicious nurses, tales of goblins and fairies being most prolific in this respect.

"The ineradicability of fears, when inculcated in early childhood, is clearly illustrated by a Southern lady who, even in advanced age, dared not go alone into the dark, although she had long ceased to believe in the stories which had made her afraid to do so. She realised this so forcibly that she would not permit her three daughters to be told any of the alarming stories which most Southern children learn. This resulted in the girls never having known what it meant to be afraid of the dark. Indeed, it was the habit of their school fellows to send them off into dark and eery places to show off their powers."

And, from one of the most experienced psychiatrists of the United States, Doctor W. A. White, superintendent of the great Government Hospital for the Insane, at Washington, we have this emphatic statement as to the general relationship between fairy tales and mental diseases:

"You will find, not infrequently, that the precipitating factors in psychoses come from the books of fairy tales which your children are allowed to feed upon."

Of course, as already intimated, a mental overthrow from the hearing or reading of fairy tales presupposes an undue impressionability on the victim's part. But how are parents to determine whether or no their children's psychic make-up is such as to render them immune from the possible mind-enfeebling effects of "horror tales"? And, in any event, let me repeat with all the emphasis at my command, there is reason to believe that no child can escape some stunting or distorting of character if brought up on a diet of ultra-sanguinary fairy tales.

As I write these lines, a stupendous war is raging in Europe with a ferocity that appals the outside world. Especially atrocious is the policy of one of the embattled nations, formerly regarded as a leader in modern civilisation. To attain its ends, this nation has violated treaty obligations as though they were of no consequence whatever; it has ruthlessly slain innocent noncombatants, even the citizens of neutral countries; wherever it has been victorious, it stands accused of vile brutalities. In its attitude towards its own soldiers it has displayed an almost incredible callousness, hurling them to certain destruction with cold-blooded nonchalance.

Beholding all this, the people of other lands marvel and question. That, in the twentieth century, even under the stress of war, a civilised nation should thus revert to barbarism seems to baffle explanation. For myself, however, I am convinced that at least a partial explanation is to be found in the fact that the offending nation is one among whom the myth, the legend, and the fairy tale have pre-eminently flourished.

In the stories which distinguished scholars have eagerly assisted to make available to the youth of this nation, indifference to human suffering and human life are too often conspicuous elements. Too often they are tinged by more than a suggestion of bloodthirstiness, cruelty, and the principle of revenge. When the childish mind has been fed upon these, stimulated by them to unhealthy fancies, and re-enforced in those instincts inherited from the primitive, which it should be the business of education to weaken and repress, is it to be wondered at that, in the crisis of war, there has been a veritable relapse to primitive savagery?

In some degree, moreover, all the warring nations have been bred on fairy tales, and, in some degree, all have exhibited the same tendency to the cruel ways of primitive man. Throughout the world a fairy tale reform is needed for the development and maintenance of a true civilisation.

But, mark you, it is a reform that is needed, not a banishment of the fairy tale. As some one has well said, a child who never hears a fairy tale is developing a tract in his soul that, in later life, will grow barren. More than this, cases are on record indicating that unless the child's instinctive craving for the romantic and the ideal is satisfied by well-chosen fairy tales, he may gratify this craving in ways that shock his elders.

I will give one instance, by way of concrete illustration. For knowledge of this I am indebted to President Hall, of Clark University, and I give it in President Hall's own words:

"Two immigrants in New York brought up their daughter, born here, on a diet of literal truth, and tabooed fiction, poetry, and imagination as lies. She was bright, at twelve had never read a fairy tale or a story book, but was continually dreamy and ardent-souled, with a great passion and talent for music. Her mother once told her that she might, perhaps, play some time to the President. Soon after, at the dedication of Grant's Tomb, she saw Mr. and Mrs. McKinley. One day, soon afterwards, she rushed in, breathless, saying that they had visited her school, heard her play, might adopt her, would give papa a place in Washington, and so on; but Mrs. McKinley was out of funds, and her husband was in Washington.

"Accordingly, Gertrude's father drew a hundred from his fortune of fourteen hundred dollars in the bank and sent it by his daughter, who brought back costly flowers. Upon more excuses, more money was loaned, and more presents were sent to Gertrude's parents—a canary, a puppy, a diamond ring. Gertrude conversed intelligently on political topics, and her father gave up his position, as he was about to accept a five-thousand-dollar job in Washington.

"Then came the crash. Gertrude had never met the President or his wife, but had made lavish presents and had bought many articles, which she had stored with a neighbour; and, to her parents' especial horror, had laid in a large stock of fairy tales and other fiction."

With justification, President Hall adds: "This points a moral against the pedagogic theory that would starve the imagination."[16]

---

[16] "Educational Problems," vol. i, pp. 359-360.

In truth, the cultivation of the imaginative faculty by means of the fairy tale is one of the great opportunities of parenthood. Only see to it that the fairy tales employed for this purpose do not reek of brutality and gore, of treachery and cunning.

And see to it that elements like these are not unduly conspicuous in any other kind of tales you put into the hands of your children. Give them no books to read, tell them no stories that may react on a sensitive mind to the development either of callousness or fear. Be careful even with regard to the tales you tell your children in the course of their religious education. Dwell on the rewards of goodness rather than on the punishments of sin. In the religious instruction of the young, as in all other instruction, over-emphasis on the grim and the terrifying may have unfavourable consequences, persisting to the end of life.

Recall, if you please, the case of the overworked Boston young man, mentioned in "Psychology and Parenthood" (p. 273). Obsessed with an idea that he had committed "the unpardonable sin," he was surely drifting to some institution for the insane, when he was fortunate enough to come under the care of a physician familiar with the new psychological discoveries and methods. Recall this young man's autobiographical statement, given to his physician, after the latter had helped him back to health:

"My abnormal fear certainly originated from doctrines of hell which I heard in early childhood, particularly from a rather ignorant elderly woman who taught Sunday-school. My early religious thought was chiefly concerned with the direful eternity of torture that might be awaiting me if I was not good enough to be saved."

You are careful as to the food you give your child's body. Be no less careful as to the food you give his mind.

CHAPTER IX

"NIGHT TERRORS"

REFERENCE has already been made more than once, though only in an incidental way, to the childhood malady of *pavor nocturnus*, or "night terrors." In any book like the present one the subject of night terrors is deserving of detailed discussion. Not only do night terrors constitute a real handicap of childhood, but also they constitute a handicap, the seriousness of which is not yet appreciated by many people, and the true nature of which is as yet known to exceedingly few. In some quarters, indeed, there has been a disposition to minimise this malady, because it usually is "outgrown" by the eighth or ninth year. But, in reality, its effects—or, rather, the effects of the condition of which it is a sign—may, and often do, continue through life. Fortunately, the new knowledge that psychology has gained concerning it enables parents to frustrate its evil consequences and, in most cases, to prevent its occurrence.

At bottom, night terrors are almost identical with the nightmares of adult years. They are, to put it precisely, juvenile nightmares, with the added feature of profound disturbance in the waking state. The one real point of difference between night terrors and nightmares is that the former indicate a greater degree of nervous strain. The child who is a victim of night terrors generally has an hour or so of quiet sleep after going to bed. Then he wakes, shrieking for his mother. When the parents, alarmed, rush to his room, they are likely to find him out of bed, crouching behind a chair, or in the corner. His eyes are staring and full of horror. He seems not to recognise his parents, though he will eagerly clutch at them for protection. After a few minutes the attack passes off, he quiets down, returns to bed, and sleeps soundly until morning, when, as a rule, he has no conscious remembrance of his fears of the night before.

While the night terror is at its height the child may have ghastly hallucinations, representing a continuance in the waking state of the dream-images that have distressed him. Also, instead of leaping out of bed, he may merely sit up, or may find it impossible to move at all, as is the case with many adults when coming out of a nightmare. A Chicago physician, describing his experiences as a child, relates:

"When I was five years of age, and during the sixth year, I suffered from nightmare. I sat up in bed and fancied I saw a monkey come down the chimney and fasten itself to my shoulder and bite me, and terrify me so that I would scream out. My older sister would then come, wake me up thoroughly, and satisfy me that it was but a vision.

"Other nights I would feel a sense of oppression, ringing in ears, a sensation of perceiving something very small, which, gradually at first, and then rapidly, assumed enormous proportions and vast whirling speed, and which, I imagined, whirled me off with it—a buzzing in my ears, probably. Then would I feel that animals—rats—would creep over me and press heavily upon me, and I could neither move hand nor foot, nor speak."

The reference to the buzzing in the ears is typical of the attitude that until lately has been taken by almost all physicians in respect both to adult and to juvenile nightmares. For that matter, it still is the attitude of those physicians who are not familiar with the findings of medical psychology. Nightmare to them, whether in the old or in the young, is altogether a question of physical causation. As they see it, one need not look beyond bodily conditions of some sort to understand the nightmares of adults and the night terrors of children. Accordingly, treatment by sedatives, dieting, and hygienic measures has been the rule. Unfortunately, this by no means always succeeds in bringing about the desired result, although such measures undoubtedly do benefit the general health.

Seemingly, to be sure, they are especially successful in the case of night terrors. But it is significant that, even if left untreated, night terrors seldom persist beyond the period of childhood. Then, however, those who have had them show a tendency, in many cases, to be troubled by unpleasant dreams, often taking on the character of most distressing nightmares. The frequency of these may, or may not, be diminished by the usual treatment of a dietetic sort. On the other hand, observation has shown that many persons afflicted with the indigestion and other physical conditions commonly held responsible for nightmares are not troubled by nightmare at all. As one observer puts it, even a person whose stomach is half destroyed by cancer may commit all sorts of dietary indiscretions and not suffer from nightmare in the slightest.

Evidently, then, physical conditions do not of themselves account for nightmares and night terrors. One must look elsewhere for their ultimate cause. This is what the medical psychologists have done, and, doing this, they have discovered that the children who are troubled by night terrors are always children of a sensitive nervous organisation who have been subjected to emotional stress. A child may be nervously highstrung, yet entirely escape night terrors, provided his mind be kept free from emotional upheavals. But let anything occur to disturb him emotionally in an excessive degree and he at once becomes likely to suffer, not only from night terrors, but also—as it has been a prime purpose of this book to impress convincingly on every reader—from nervous affections of a more serious kind. He may even have "day terrors," seeing imaginary and terrifying objects as vividly as the child who wakes in panic from a distressing dream.

For example, a boy of eight was sent to the Washington neurologist, Doctor T. A. Williams, to be treated for general nervousness, and, in particular, for a tendency "to see things where there is really nothing to be seen." Doctor Williams found the boy to be so nervous that it was hard for him to sit still and to keep from wriggling excitedly about in his chair. Questioned as to his hallucinations, he said that these were mostly of a snake. He could not describe the imaginary snake, except to say that its head was like an eel's. It seemed to come from nowhere, and presented itself to his astonished gaze with a suddenness that caused him to scream and run. His father gave Doctor Williams the additional information that these hallucinations were experienced only when the boy was alone, and that, though his day terrors were not followed by night terrors, he would not go to bed unless some one were in the room with him.

Questioning his little patient more closely, Doctor Williams next learned that he had a veritable horror of being alone at any time. As long as somebody was in sight, he could enjoy his games, and would readily run errands. Left alone, the imaginary snake, or some hallucinatory wild beast, was almost at once seen by him. Further inquiry brought out the significant fact that this fear of solitude had actually been implanted in the boy by over-anxiety on his mother's part.

His horror of being alone was paralleled by her dread of having him out of her sight. She was continually thinking, and talking, of risks he would incur if he were allowed to be by himself. In this way she had unconsciously infected him with a "fixed idea" that something dreadful was sure to happen to him unless older persons were at hand to protect him. This fixed idea preying on his unusually impressionable mind, and keeping him in a constant state of emotional strain, was the decisive factor in the production of his day terrors. In proof whereof it need only be added that his hallucinations and general nervousness ceased to trouble him soon after corrective training was begun, supplemented by treatment by "suggestion" to rid him of the abnormal fear of being alone.

Fortunately, though I might detail a number of other cases of day terrors, this affliction is of rare occurrence, compared with night terrors. And, from the point of view of the medical psychologist, it is only to be expected that such should be the case. As explained by Doctor Williams, in a passage which gives a clear idea of the mechanism of night terrors:

"If I say to a small boy that a bear will eat him up, the effect upon his emotions entirely differs, whether I make the remark with portentous gravity and horror, or whether I say it with bubbling joviality as, evidently, a huge joke. In the first eventuality, the boy will rush to my side in terror and try to be saved from the bear, and a phobia is in course of construction; with the latter proceeding, the boy will laugh consumedly, and it would not take much to make him enter the cage and strike the bear. But, even when terrified, a child feels a refuge in the protection of his elders during the day, when they are rarely absent. . . .

"At night, however, the child is alone, and his little consciousness cannot find the support of others. Before the kaleidoscope of his dreams pass the various images and accompanying emotions of his waking life, so that if any of these images has become linked with fear it is certain to bring with it terror, as it surges into dream in the night, and the child jumps up, awakened, in panic, finding no one near, upon whom to lean."[17]

[17] *Archives of Pediatrics*, December, 1914.

In many a case of night terrors, no great psychological skill is required to detect the influence of emotional stress as the prime factor in causing the alarming attacks. In one instance that has come to my knowledge, a seven-year-old girl was brought to a physician, with a history of both night and day terrors. She was subject, her mother said, to attacks of loud screaming, during which she seemed dazed and in an agony of fear. The attacks sometimes lasted ten minutes, and immediately afterwards the girl generally fell into a heavy sleep. Her night terrors were of the usual sort, except that on the occasion of the first attack she was in such a panic that she opened her bedroom window and threw herself out of it. Luckily, it was early evening, and her mother, walking in the garden beneath her window, was able to catch her and save her from harm.

"She had gone to bed as usual," the mother said, in detailing this episode, "and seemed to be quite well, though I remember I thought she looked a little wild about the eyes. For an hour she slept quietly. Then, as I later learned, she woke up moaning, jumped out of bed, and made for the window."

"And," asked the physician to whom the child had been taken, "had anything out of the way occurred to her that day?"

"Nothing."

"Are you sure of that?"

"Well, nothing of real account, at all events. I have been told that somebody jokingly said to her that if she were not a good girl a black man would come to her room and carry her off. But this did not seem to disturb her much at the time."

Hereupon, the situation became clear to the physician. It was evident that, subconsciously if not consciously, the thought of the supposed danger, acting on a mind none too well organised by inheritance—there was epilepsy in the family—had acquired sufficient force to bring on the attack of nocturnal panic and the subsequent attacks of day and night terrors. Probably, moreover, this was not the first time that statements of a fear-inspiring character had been made to the child, so that this last "joke" might well serve to agitate her excessively.

Compare with this the case of a four-year-old boy, whose night terrors were accompanied by a strange hallucination that he saw the devil, and that the devil was trying to catch him. Every night for several weeks he would wake after one or two hours of sleep, would leap from bed with a shriek, and run wildly around the room, calling on his mother to save him and to drive the devil out of the house.

Impressed by the recurrence of this hallucination, the physician in charge of the case questioned the boy's mother as to a possible explanation for his believing the devil was chasing him. Reluctantly, the mother confessed that one day when her little son had been unruly she had warned him that if he did not behave the devil would come for him. It was the night after she had thus foolishly threatened him that he had his first attack of *pavor nocturnus*. Armed with this knowledge, the physician began a course of treatment which effected a cure in a week. It properly included tonics and dieting to overcome the indigestion and other physical ailments caused by the strain of nervous excitement. But its principal feature was treatment by suggestion, to dislodge from the boy's mind his morbid fear of the devil.

Anything which causes the instinct of fear to function abnormally may act with decisive force in bringing on night terrors. The telling of ghost stories and other gruesome tales of the supernatural has been productive of much harm in this respect. And, as brought out in the preceding chapter, cases of night terrors have similarly been traced to the hearing or reading by children of fairy tales containing elements of the horrible. The child that is supersensitive may be so impressed by these elements as to brood over them and, in waking reverie, apply them to himself. Thus they get fixed in the mind, to disturb and alarm it, and, eventually, to find expression in dreams of so unpleasant a character that night terrors may be a result.

With the night terrors left untreated psychologically, subsequent nervous ailments, perhaps lifelong invalidism, may further penalise the hapless victim of parental thoughtlessness. I am reminded of a certain patient of Doctor Sidis's, a woman afflicted with neurotic ills up to the age of sixty, and, when she first consulted the New England specialist, displaying a most complicated set of disease symptoms. She had kidney trouble, stomach trouble, frequent headaches, insomnia, and general nervousness. In especial, she suffered from an obsessive fear of becoming insane. This fear, at times, was so extreme that she would walk up and down her room night after night, "like an animal in a cage," to use Doctor Sidis's expressive phrase. Repeated examinations by different physicians had failed to bring to light any evidences of organic disease of stomach, kidneys, or brain, and a diagnosis of hysteria had finally been made. Consequently, it became Doctor Sidis's special task to endeavour to get at these latent memory-images that had acted with disintegrative power on the mental and bodily processes, recall them to conscious remembrance, and, by suggestive treatment, rob them of their disease-producing potency.

Step by step, by a method of psychological analysis of his own invention, he took his patient back through her life history. He found that, in middle life, she had had several distressing experiences, but none of them adequate to account for her hysteria. Always, there remained an obscure element which did not become clearly outlined until, in the course of the analysis, childhood memories began to emerge. Then it appeared that there had been a period of night terrors, the source of which was definitely traced to a shock experienced at the age of five. At that age, through some mischance, the patient had been allowed to spend some time with an insane woman who was in a maniacal state.

Of a sensitive nervous organisation to begin with, she was overwhelmed by this experience. She could not get the image of the insane woman out of her mind, and the fearful thought kept coming again and again to her, "Do little girls ever go insane?" Then followed the night terrors, to be "outgrown" in due course. But the analysis revealed that, though the memory of her experience with the insane woman had gradually faded from conscious recollection, it had never been subconsciously forgotten. Even now, fifty-five years later, she still saw this woman in her dreams. It was the baneful influence of this shock that had given rise to her obsessive fear of insanity and had prepared the ground for the condition of abnormal suggestibility making possible the hysterical imitation of organic kidney and stomach disease. As was proved by the outcome of Doctor Sidis's psychotherapeutic treatment.

Now the question comes: If night terrors are so portentous a danger-signal, how prevent the development of the mentally disturbed and nervously strained condition which they indicate? This question has, perhaps, been sufficiently answered in previous chapters. Here I would simply reaffirm that emotional control is the great object to be kept steadily in view. It is, indeed, significant that night terrors are most likely to appear in children having a nervous, excitable father or mother. The emotionality, the chronic worrying and anxiety of the parent infect the child by the power of psychic contagion and make him fall an easy prey to any disquieting experience.

And if, despite well-ordered moral training and the benign influence of a good parental example, the child shows a tendency to develop night terrors—what then? Well, here is how one psychologically enlightened parent nipped in the bud a fear-bred condition that might have resulted in night terrors or in some specific nervous ailment of the waking life:

"For several weeks my boy, three and a half years old, had been visiting the zoölogical garden every afternoon, in the company of a French maid of exceptionally forceful character, and apparently free from the superstitiousness of the average nurse. For a long time all went well, until one evening the boy began to cry soon after he was left for the night. At this unusual occurrence, I mounted the stairs and inquired the cause of the boy's trouble.

"He said there were lions in the house and that he did not want to stay alone, as he was afraid they would eat him. The source of the idea had been that the lions had roared more loudly than usual on that particular afternoon, and he had been much impressed, standing for some time quite motionless before the cage, though terrified. I soon convinced the boy that the lions had to remain in their cages, and could not get out; hence, there were none in the house, so that there was no occasion to fear. Of course, it was first necessary to give him the feeling of security gained by embracing me; and, secondly, to begin the conversation by talking of something else—I have forgotten what.

"In this way the state of terror was dismissed, and the feeling of protection was induced before we returned to the subject of the lions. Then we made rather a joke of the funny roaring of the lions before we had finished, and he finally lay down, with the solemn purpose to go to sleep and think, as I suggested, of the tramcars and motors passing outside his open window. It was all very simple substitution, but it was the prevention of what might have become a serious fear-psychosis if injudiciously handled."[18]

It should be added that special need for training in emotional control is indicated if a child begins to be troubled, not by night terrors, but by another and more common childhood malady—somnambulism. The child who talks or walks

[18] *Archives of Pediatrics,* December, 1914.

in his sleep, like the child attacked by night terrors, is, for some reason, nervously unstrung; and, it may confidently be said, is usually unstrung because of the presence in his mind of disquieting ideas, conscious or subconscious. On this account, the parent should not be satisfied with the measures ordinarily employed in dealing with both night terrors and somnambulism—the prescribing of tonics and sedatives, outdoor exercise, abstinence from tea and coffee, reduction in meat in the diet, and so forth. Undeniably, these measures often result in a complete cessation of the nocturnal symptoms. But, even if, as a result of medication, exercise, and dieting, the disquieting ideas causing the symptoms no longer manifest their presence by the attacks that have alarmed the parents, these ideas still are left in the mind, perchance to cause still more alarming symptoms later. Accordingly, the really prudent parent, besides dieting his child, will endeavour to get at the mental source of trouble.

Sometimes he can do this by closely observing the behaviour of the child in his waking moments, and the trend of his waking thoughts. Or he can do it by gaining the child's confidence and questioning him as to any fears, worries, or griefs that may be disturbing him. If, as will often happen, the child insists, it may be in all sincerity, that nothing is troubling him, there is yet another avenue of information open to the parent—namely, by questioning the child about his dreams. Through studying his dreams, in fact, it is possible to gain clearer insight into his mental life than perhaps by any other means.

Again and again, as we have seen, the modern psychologist has made use of dream-analysis with illuminating results. Parents can and should similarly analyse their children's dreams. And I feel justified in predicting that parents of the future, alert to detect and correct any undesirable trends in their children's mental and moral development, will make frequent use of dream-analysis as an aid in successful child-rearing.

The helpfulness of dream-analysis to parents comes from the fact that the dreams of children usually relate either to things which the children dread, or things which they desire. This is also true of the dreams of adults, as shown by the analysis of thousands of dreams. In the case of adults, however, the fear or the desire mirrored by the dream is nearly always masked by the variety and seeming absurdity or incongruity of the dream-images. As when, for example, a complicated, fantastic dream of adventure in an out-of-the-way part of the world is found, on examination, to be connected with a secret longing for marriage. Accordingly, prolonged and tedious analysis is often needed to get at the true meaning of an adult's dreams. In the case of children's dreams, the opposite is the rule. There is little repression or distortion, the dream dealing directly with what is uppermost in the dreamer's waking mind, and emphasising the fears or fulfilling the wishes of his waking life.

This is what makes dream-analysis both easy and profitable to parents. Once aware of the wish-fulfilling rôle of dreams, no parent need experience difficulty in interpretation if his small boy reports to him a series of dreams like the following:

"It was after school, and I went with other boys to a candy store, and the storekeeper told us we could have anything we wanted. We had a fine time. I filled my pockets with chocolates and caramels and peanut candy, besides what I ate while I was in the store.

"I was at a party, and there was plenty to eat and drink. We had sandwiches and lemonade, ice cream and cake. After it was over, they told us we could take away all the food that was not eaten.

"There was a fire in the next street, and I went to see the firemen at work. It was rainy and cold, and somebody brought out coffee and cake for the firemen. There was more than they could eat, so they gave me some."

Dreamed by a small boy living in a poor home, dreams like these would be of a pathetic, rather than sinister, import. For they would represent the imaginary fulfilment of wishes unrealisable in the waking life, and would thus be a subconscious protest against the cramping limitations of poverty. Even so, whether the youthful dreamer were the son of poor parents or the son of parents comfortably circumstanced, it would be an unescapable inference that, when awake, he was inclined to think overmuch of his stomach. Wherefore, dreams like these, if dreamed with any frequency, would unmistakably suggest the desirability of training to check a tendency to gluttony and greed.

The frequency with which dreams of a given type are dreamed has, indeed, much to do with their significance as indicators of character defects. An occasional dream of gorging one's self—or, say, of being the centre of attraction at an evening party—would not be valid ground for indicting a little boy of greed, or a little girl of vanity. But, if such dreams are habitual, or if, despite a seeming variety in the dreams reported by son or daughter, there is discernible an undercurrent of desires incompatible with strength and beauty of character, then the wise parent will not delay in supplementing dream study by educational measures to correct the indicated defects.

And, as emphasised by the experiences of many of the youthful nervous patients whose case-histories have been given in this book, dream-analysis should particularly be utilised to help children who—being free from adenoids, eye-strain, or other adverse physical conditions—show a sudden and unfavourable change in disposition. Some cause of emotional stress is undoubtedly present, and it may be taken for granted that the child will betray, through the content of his dreams, what is troubling his mind. Dream-analysis will thus give insight into secret jealousies, secret desires, secret fears, secret mental conflicts of many kinds, that are provocative both of unfavourable changes in character and of outright ill health.

One such conflict, to which I have already referred when discussing the handicap of sulkiness, is conflict over sex questions. Frequently, to the parents' astonishment, it will be found that the actual cause of timidity, reticence, moodiness, or depression of spirits in a formerly happy child, is a mental conflict due to the child's vain endeavours to work out fully satisfactory answers to delicate questions which the parents have not answered when put to them by the child, or have answered in an evasive fashion. Children are far more discerning than most parents give them credit for being. Also, they often are more interested than most parents suppose in some of the fundamental problems of existence—and especially the problem of their own nature and origin. The scientific study of dreams, indeed, has furnished an additional and powerful argument against the common practice among parents of veiling in mystery or concealing with well-intentioned falsehoods the facts of birth and of sex.

But let me quote, at this point, the findings of an English medical psychologist, Doctor Ernest Jones, of London, who has specially studied the reactions of children to the policy of silence and mystification regarding sex matters.

"The extent to which such matters occupy the mind of the young child," says Doctor Jones, "is always underestimated by adults, and is impossible to determine by a casual examination, for, on the one hand, the later memories for these years are always deficient and erroneous, and, on the other hand, this aspect of the child's mind is rarely accessible to direct inquiry, on account of the barrier always existing on the subject between child and adult. As the child grows older, the desires and tendencies in question meet with such obstacles as an increasing sense of shame, guilt, wrongness, remorse, and so on, and are fought against by the child, who now half-consciously strives to get away from them, to forget them, or, as it is technically termed, to "repress" them. The repressed mental processes are later thus forgotten, and, along with them, a major part of the mental experiences associated with them in time. This is the reason why so little of early childhood life can be recalled by the adult.

"The desires, thoughts, impulses, tendencies, and wishes thus repressed do not, however, die; they live on, but come to expression in other forms. Their energy is directed along more useful paths, a process known as "sublimation," and upon the extent and kind of this sublimation depends a great deal of the future interests and activities of the individual."[19]

Under certain conditions, instead of smooth, successful sublimation, there may be mental conflict, with nervous or mental maladies as a possible result. To this undesirable outcome the parental course sometimes contributes materially. Again, I quote Doctor Jones:

"It is almost a regular occurrence for children of the age of four or five to turn from their parents, to withdraw into themselves, and to pursue private speculations about the topics concerning which they have been denied information, whether by a direct refusal or by evasion. Phantasies of bitter resentment against the parent commonly occur at this time, and often form the basis not only of a later want of confidence, or even a more or less veiled hostility as regards the parents, but also of various subsequent disharmonies, neurotic disturbances, and so forth."

Of course, readers of these pages scarcely need to be reminded, conflict over questions of birth and sex is only one form of emotional stress that may occasion night terrors, somnambulism, changes in character, and unmistakable nervous ailments. Whatever the stress, it will be indicated by the child's dreams, either directly or symbolically. Which, of itself, is abundant reason for parents to gain knowledge of at least the chief principles of scientific dream-interpretation.

[19] *The Journal of Educational Psychology*, November, 1910.

CHAPTER X

IN CONCLUSION

FROM what has been said in the foregoing pages, it is an irresistible inference that the greatest of all handicaps a child can have, short of being born hopelessly deficient, is to be born into a home where he will be exposed to mind-deadening or emotion-stressing influences—a home where he will receive neither adequate mental stimulus nor adequate moral training. Under such circumstances, so profound is the influence of the early environment, his growth to a normal manhood is impossible, unless other and more favourable influences from outside the home affect him with sufficient force to offset the home surroundings. Fortunately, this happens in many cases, but, as hospital, asylum, and court records testify in sad abundance, in many cases the adverse home environment proves indeed decisive.

And, on the opposite, that child is unquestionably getting the best possible start in life who is born of parents appreciative of his mental needs, sincerely devoted to him, but not over-devoted, watchful of his physical health and alert to prevent him from becoming a slave to his emotions. The purpose of both this book and its predecessor, "Psychology and Parenthood," has been to help this latter class of parents and, perchance, to awaken other parents to the need for giving more care and intelligent attention to their children than they have hitherto been doing.

Certainly, the discoveries of modern psychology and physiology have made it increasingly evident that the business of child-rearing is, of all businesses, far and away the most important to the race. And it is a business that has become more important than it ever was in the past, because of the greater demands made on human mentality, and the more numerous sources of stress on human emotionality that are involved in the increasing complexity of civilised life. Either the clock of progress must be stopped and the world revert to more primitive modes of living, or else the men and women of the days to come must be conditioned, through wiser educational methods that begin in the first years of life, to adapt themselves more smoothly to the modern environment.

We do not want to stop the clock of progress. But neither could we wish to see the people of the world degenerate into a race of psychasthenes, neurasthenes, and otherwise mentally or nervously disorganised men and women. Happily, means of attaining smoother adaptation, of increasing both the mental vigour and the nervous resistance of the race are now available. They are available, thanks chiefly to the labours of the medical psychologists. And it is my hope that, by stressing the adaptatory elements in their discoveries and presenting them concretely to the lay reader, I may have contributed something to promote appreciation of these elements by parents in general, and appropriate action for the benefit of the growing generation. First and last, be it clearly understood, it is on the development of a really efficient parenthood that the future of society depends.

INDEX

P

R

S

T

U

W

Printed by Libri Plureos GmbH in Hamburg,
Germany